BLACK CAT IN THE WINDOW

Liam Ó Murchú has had a varied career as a public servant, broadcaster and writer. Now retired he still 'tends his flock', i.e. continues to write. He is noted for achieving the impossible by making Irish on television acceptable in popular entertainment.

BLACK CAT IN THE WINDOW

Liam Ó Murchú

The Collins Press

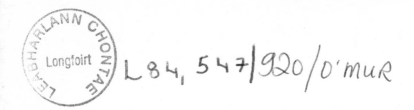
Published in 1999 by
The Collins Press
West Link Park
Doughcloyne
Wilton
Cork

British Library Cataloguing in Publication data.

Typesetting by The Collins Press Ltd.

Printed in Ireland by Colour Books Ltd.

ISBN: 1-898256-85-3

CONTENTS

❧

PROLOGUE

Two hundred years ago, the poet William Blake was writing his *Songs of Innocence and Experience*. The 'Songs of Innocence' saw the good, cheerful side of life; the 'Songs of Experience' saw the same things but with a colder, more objective eye. The little chimney-sweep climbing through the black and choking soot is a happy-go-lucky chap, bright and chirpy as the sparrows in the nest he comes upon in his climb; the eight year-old going down the mine-shaft or greasing the engine in one of those 'dark satanic mills' sings songs of innocence when paid his penny stipend at the week's end. But the horrors of the soot-black hell, the death and maiming of mill and mine-shaft – those were what the songs of experience were about. The victims of both must never rest till they have wiped them clean from the face of the earth and built 'a new Jerusalem in England's green and pleasant land'.

The story here is about another country and happens two centuries after Blake's time. What's more, the world has gone a further full circle since then – in Ireland more than most countries on earth. But it is still present, the living moment that is fixed in all our memories – when what was is, when the 'I' that was becomes the 'I' that is, that still-frame moment held and transfixed now and for all eternity.

In such a moment, we live our life as it is happening; the songs of innocence and the songs of experience merge and become one, to make that 'still sad music of humanity' which, for past, present and future, is the story of us all.

These are some of the songs of the early years of mine.

1

The Bells of Shandon

THERE is a large floor of broken boards, covered here and there with bits and pieces of linoleum. I am sitting in the middle. I cannot see the walls or what's above them, but there is a woman at a fire who keeps looking at me and a man on a chair reading a paper, who keeps looking at me too. There is a smell of something frying in a pan which is a good smell; the reason I know it's good is that the man and woman are saying so and I know they must be right because they always are. They are my father and my mother. I do not know what 'my father' and 'my mother' mean. I do not know what any words mean; all I know is that there is a light in their eyes and it's on me and it's the thing that keeps me safe. Safe is about the last thing I should feel in this terrible place.

Down on the other floors below us there are other people. I know their names. First, there are the Goods, Winnie and Willie; they own the house and we pay rent to them. They have a thing called a laundry in the basement where people come and go all the time. It has great big baskets full of clothes, but sometimes they are not full and could easily hold a child, hold several children, who could be stifled or choked there, though that's not what they're supposed to be for. Winnie and Willie are nice but when they ask me and my big sister to come in and tell us they have something good for us to eat, we're always afraid to go because they could grab us and shove us in one of the baskets and pull the lid down and leave us there to fatten until it's time to take us and boil us and gobble us up, like the wicked witch did with the children in the story. Winnie is big and has red cheeks and Willie is small and fat. They have no children of their own; that's why they want us. They're always trying to lure us in with sweets and cakes and slices of bread and jam – only it's not jam, it's a horrible yellow thing called 'marmalade', which has bits of orange-skins stuck in it. We hate it but pretend to like it because our mother says we must be nice to them, especially when she can't pay the rent.

The rent is a big thing in our mother's life and we know it. So we put the bread-and-marmalade to our mouths and try to eat but we can't, it's pure poison – so we take it away again and, the first chance we get, we run off and hide it in the tall grass of the green outside the front door. And then we make for the safety of our own place on the fourth floor.

Only it's not safe getting there either. The first landing is not too bad. That's where Miss Goggin lives; she has cats and only at night is it scary. Then the cats are out and they're always letting horrible shrieks and howls out of them, as if someone is trying to strangle or choke them. Maybe someone is. But then, when we look, it's only other cats and they're shrieking and howling too. For things that are supposed to be pets, they make an awful sound.

But Miss Goggin herself is nice. She has bright flowery curtains on the window and her two chairs are covered the same. It's like a real lady's house. That's what she is, 'a lady'; she wears a hat and coat when she goes out, not like all the other women. They wear shawls. The shawls are black and thick and they have lovely soft tassels which you can pull off and chew – only not while Mother is around; she'd kill you. There are lots of things you cannot do while Mother is around. She'd never try to lure you into a laundry basket with bread-and-marmalade and she'd never shriek and howl like Miss Goggin's cats but one black look from her is enough to stop us doing whatever we're doing.

The third landing, the one below us, is the worst. That's where Annie Downey lives, the living terror of our lives. Everyone says she's mad, with her hair wild and her big teeth and the eyes jumping out of her head. But Mother says 'Miss Downey' is only a lonely poor soul and we're not to be afraid passing her door, even though she may be a small bit cracked and 'astray in the head'. That doesn't do us any good at all when we're passing her door. The door is always open, and we know she's in there, ready to pounce. The stairs creak under our feet and we think it's Mad Annie and we shout for Mother to open our own door so we can see our way up. She does too – which is just as well because now we're three flights up and we'll jump all the way if she comes out.

But then Mother goes back into our own place, leaving us all alone in the dark again – only this time we hear her calling down to us from inside: 'Come on up, will ye? What's the matter with ye? Isn't Miss Downey there? She'll mind ye.'

What strange, stupid things mothers can say!

There must be others in this house as well as those. It's a great big block of a place – but those are the ones we know. And our place on the fourth landing must be more than one room because our mother and father are there and the six of us. There were six more but they died.

The big windows look out on the Green Garden which has railings all around it. Across the road there's a baker's shop with the name 'Simcox' over the door. It's the first word I will ever write. I trace the shape of the letters on the glass of the fogged-up window, my nose pressed against the glass until it freezes. The window, the house, the baker's shop will all be gone one day and our mother says 'not before their time' – but I do not know that now. All I know is that it is there and the shape and make of it for me will never change. It is at the foot of Shandon Street and Blarney Street in the city of Cork in the south of Ireland, a fork in the road called 'Goulnaspurra'. That's from the Irish 'Gabhal na Spurra', 'the fork of the spur'. I'll learn that from the Christian Brothers of St Columba's, Blarney Street later on.

The clock-tower of Shandon is a little way up the road from us and it has bells which ring the quarter hours. Sometimes, if there are visitors up there, the man in the bell-tower will play lovely airs for them, airs that I will later learn are 'Moore's Melodies': 'The Minstrel Boy', 'Oft in the Stilly Night', 'Believe Me If All Those Endearing Young Charms'. They never play our own air, 'The Banks of My Own Lovely Lee'. Maybe that's because when the river is low, the smell can be bad and they don't want to remind people of it.

But what I can't understand is why they don't play the air we all know so well which tells the story of those very bells:

> With deep affection
> And recollection,

The Bells of Shandon

I often think of
　　Those Shandon bells,
Whose sounds so wild would
In the days of childhood,
Fling round my cradle
　　Their magic spells.
On this I ponder
Where'er I wander,
And thus grow fonder,
　　Sweet Cork, of thee;
With thy bells of Shandon
That sound so grand on
The pleasant waters
　　Of the river Lee.

Grand indeed they do sound, especially on a fine summer night when there is still light in the sky and we don't need to light the paraffin lamp. Not that the light of the paraffin lamp isn't nice too; it's like the light upon me from my father's and mother's eyes when they think I'm not looking. I know then that we have nothing, but I know too that we have everything. Everything is having things to eat and drink and having people around to love and mind you.

Not that there aren't bad things too. There's no water, no lav; only an open fire to cook on and nowhere to hang the clothes when they're wet. Mother says these are bad things and they'll be the death of her. But one of these days, she says, it's all going to change; she's going to get this new house in a new place and we'll say goodbye to all that. But for now it's this and the fire is lighting, and there are three bars across it through which the red coals glow, and when she takes the steaming kettle from the hook and pours the water into the zinc tub to wash our clothes, we stand around and wait for her to be finished because then it's our turn to be washed. Then, we're up to our necks in soapy water which, even if it's dirty itself, is a lot cleaner than we are, and by the time we come out we're as clean as new pins, which we think is a sore thing to be, but she says no matter, we're never to get as dirty as that again.

Sometimes there are fights on the steps beside the Green Garden and bad enough they are. The men are always drunk and they swing at each other and miss and then they go hurtling down the steps and bang against the wall, a big heavy thud we can hear from our window four flights up. But when they don't miss; it's worse. Then the fists hit faces and great heavy lurching bodies go pulling and tearing each other till they're fit to kill.

'Pet' Horgan is supposed to be a great fighter, with his big red face and the cap on the side of his head, but from what I can see he's good at only the one thing and that's getting hit himself. 'Bring out yeer fighting men now!' he roars as he staggers up the steps, and out they come, men in shirtsleeves or no sleeves at all, only a singlet on brawny shoulders, sometimes not even that but stripped to the waist like the braves in Cowboys and Indians with hatchets and tomahawks looking for skulls to sink them in. It isn't hatchets or tomahawks they have but knives and cut-throat razors; when they come out, anything can happen. The women are the worst. 'Burly Con' runs over from Coppingers Lane; he's one of the fighting men 'Pet' Horgan is shouting at to come and fight him, and he's bad enough. But then comes Mrs Burly, his wife, if that's what she is, a half-starved wild creature with black hair flying in the wind and mad with rage and drink to hit whatever is left standing after Burly has gone.

Easily the most terrible part of all this is our own mother, who can't stand the sight of people maiming each other. When they're at their worst, she'll fly out of the room and run down the stairs, right into the middle of all the murder and knives and roaring she'll go, tearing at the fighting men and pulling them apart. And I'm there at the window looking down at her, knowing she could get killed, for she's only a slip of a woman and they are great big brutes – drunken brutes at that – but nothing will stop her; in she goes, pulling, tearing, holding them apart with some extraordinary power that can't be her own, until some other women come along (it's always women) and between them they drag the men away.

Then suddenly, as quick as it started, it's all over and peace descends again. Mother comes back up, she turns down the wick on the paraffin lamp and the light goes out.

And then we all settle down to sleep to the sound of the bells of Shandon ringing the quarter hours until there isn't another sound till the sounds of a newborn day.

What is this place? What is this time? And who am I that I come to be here to live in it? My light of life upon the world cannot have been greeted with much ecstasy, though I am reliably informed that 'half-a-tierce of stout' was drunk at my christening. Rarely can a child have been less wanted: Mother was forty-six, Father two years older. With eleven squalling proofs of love's old sweet song behind them, they cannot have looked with favour upon this twelfth intruder. Had they known it, they would have understood the meaning of Scott Fitzgerald's lines:

> This is the way the world goes,
> The rich get richer, the poor get – children!

Unbidden to the feast I may have been, but that did not in the least inhibit my insistence on being there. The insistence, though not expressed in words, was abundantly clear in the howls my outsize lungs inflicted on our narrow home. To this, no fewer than three mothers would testify: a grandmother who lived nearby and was always in and out of the house; my own mother; and my disabled sister, then twenty and from an accident of childhood condemned to walk with difficulty for the rest of her life. I will come to all three later on.

My arrival meant one more mouth to feed, another foot upon the treadmill of unending work for little pay or no pay at all, and that at a time far worse than anything we have known since. Yet it is a fact that, however poor the place, a child once born was hugely welcomed into such homes, was indeed in constant danger of being all but devoured, so surely would it become the heart and centre of the house – as was certainly the case with me.

From early on, I have this thing which comes down on me when I'm asleep. It's a great swelling thing which begins to swing and whirl inside my head. It gets bigger and bigger, and thicker and faster; the whole world gets caught up in its wild and terrible beat. Then, just as it's about to explode and burst in pieces, and me with it, I wake up screaming and struggling to break out of it and get free. The whole house is in a turmoil, with women running about with crucifixes and medals, and holy water being flung all over the place, until at last I am hushed and hugged and lulled back to sleep, and the house settles down again in a fog of feathered night-shade.

In those threatened and terrifying moments, my young heart begins to know strange things; though blind to all else about me, I begin to become the at once imperilled and protected thing I am. And from then, too, I date a special bond with my disabled sister who, though useless in the world as I am, fulfils a unique and necessary purpose in my life.

What was the scene and what was the situation in Ireland then? That February day when I was born was a time of new hope in our lives. There had been a civil war following the gaining of national independence; some of the brave men who had won it for us and who should have lived to build the country up, had died in it. But for the first time in several centuries the land and resources of Ireland were being used for the country's good after years of exploitation. A small beginning – but a beginning just the same which with time could lead to better things.

Remote from all this, living our 'lives of quiet desperation', all unknown to us we had become children of a new nation. So, when on that early spring morning which thrust me naked upon the world, my younger sister Lil peeped across the cot-side and said, 'He eye-dee-open'; what his eyes opened upon was that fractious, brawling, half-starved, wildly energetic but largely unemployed slum-folk living around us in our tenement rooms, born now to a new dawn of freedom and with new horizons of freedom being opened up. The red sandstone earth was being torn up for the foundations of the town on Gurranabraher (from the Irish, 'Garrán na Bráthar', 'Garden of the Monks') atop the brow of our northside hills.

Women from the slums dreamed of such places where they would have a house of their own – 'Oh, a glassy palace we'll have, love, with our own lav and water and a black-lead polished stove to cook on!' Bliss was it upon that dawn to be alive – but the key to such a house was very heaven! The rotten mattresses dumped in the back lanes, the grime and soot of the open fires giving way to curtains of white lace and a green garden beyond, strange names and new places worthy of the dreams our mother had for us children – hopes and dreams her dreamy man had filled her with long before the harsh world caught up with him and he dropped such foolishness for good. From then on, the brawling and drunkenness would cease, the smells of woodrot and the rot of creatures, animal and human, the hundred Hogarthian lives packed and crushed into a small space – all that would cease and in their place would be the smell of new linoleum and fresh new paint, with a white deal table and chairs to match, instead of the orange and butter-boxes we had up to that, and the children would grow up to be good clean boys and girls, later men and women, schooled in the book-knowledge that would win a place for them in the bright new world.

Week by week, Mother trudged over to the City Hall to plead with toadies become high and mighty with office to get herself a notch higher on the waiting-list. She had a case: six children in a tenement house four flights up, no light but the paraffin lamp, no lav but the bucket, no water but a single tap four floors down in the basement-yard. It took time. The lists were full; incredibly, there were others who could always plead a harder case. She would come back then trailing her shawl behind her and her heart behind that again. But life went on; the insistent treadmill had to be trod and there was no let-up. The poet could sing for all he was worth that 'God's in his heaven, all's right with the world', but that was a world far, far distant from the world we lived in.

I see it all, I live in it. I hate it because our Mother hates it, and whatever she hates we hate, whatever she loves we love. What she loves is us and, like the tigress she is, will fight to the death for us.

And if we could but know it, we love her and want to be with her in this, the only world we know. Lost in the world we may be – but we are set to ride its star.

It was good, though, when the horses came up the hill, great loads piled on drays behind them, their demented drivers goading them on to gain a foothold on the rutted road. Father, whose hero-worship of his old war-comrades has not abated, has picked as godfather for me a relative, one Tygeen (the Irish for Timmy), who had been with the cavalry in Flanders. What 'being with the cavalry' meant was flogging spent mares and stallions gone beyond further use through the morasses of No Man's Land, with 'Big Berthas' of cannon loaded up behind them – good training for the carter he was to become when he got back home to Lloyd George's 'land fit for heroes' when it was all over.

My own sense of hero-worship leaps alive with pride when I see Tygeen make a run at the hill on top of his loaded dray. If he gets a good run, they can very nearly make it, but by then the horses are exhausted, with the worst still to come. There is a moment of taut and deadly danger then as Tygeen jumps down from the shaft and gets in beside them, in under them, the foaming bridles in one hand, the short whip in the other, running along in threesome with them, urging them on. It's a wild mad world then of frothing, foaming horse and man, flesh and bone and blood, of muscle, mind and skill, flints sparking the road under the plunging hooves, the great Clydesdales black with sweat, the veins bulging on their sides, and my Ben Hur god-father under them in terror of one thing and one thing only: that the horses will slip and fall and bring the slim grip he has upon the world crashing down around him on the road.

It sometimes happens. Then the horses have to be untackled, and when the bits are out and the straddles off there's no controlling the frightened, frothing beasts. Great hooves go flying wildly, looking for a purchase on the rutted road, and the men who come to help scatter like frightened birds as the panting giants, eyes frantic, nostrils wide with fright, lie hunched and helpless against the next assault.

Sometimes a leg gets broken in the attempt to get them up; then the horse has to be shot. For my cavalry godfather, that's the final blow. He just stands there, lank and helpless, waiting for the Guards with the humane killer to come up from the Bridewell near the North Gate Bridge. Then, it's the round muzzle to the horse's head, the dull hollow thud, the twitching and shivering as the struggling creature dies all over, the weight of the dray tightening upon the tangled tackle, garrotting its giant limbs in a dozen places.

Looking on at all this is another relative, my Uncle Johnny, who has lost a leg in that war of Father's they're always talking about. That put him out of action for good: now he has no option but to sit with his thoughts and his empty trouser-leg ... 'Cast a cold eye On life, on death, Horseman, pass by!'

All he can do is pity Tygeen – and what pity can be left in a man who has battered out the last of his strength in an even more senseless struggle a long time before? Such is the devil's work in these things that sometimes at such moments up the hill comes Dr Hearne, the Protestant bishop, a kindly man everyone likes but who fits ill into this scene, murmuring words of comfort about a man's duty to King and Country and blessed be the holy will of God. My one-legged Uncle Johnny nods in mute but furious acquiescence:

Tygeen's horse dead on the roadway and his own empty trouser-leg say things about the will of God that make it a very different thing in the world to which he belongs.

But life goes on in our fastness at the top of the dark stairs. There I am at the window like Robbie Burns' 'child amang ye takin' notes' – only it's not notes, it's that 'Simcox' traced out on the grimy fogged-up glass. Across the road at the foot of Shandon Street is a dark hole smelling of tanned leather and burning thong-wax. There works the cobbler, Dan Hurley, an angry ugly Rumpelstiltskin of a man, black as hell and fierce as the devil. He slides like an adder up and down off his cobbler's stool and whets his knife on a leather apron that bears the marks of a thousand cuts.

Politics, the opium of the poor, is our constant and our delight. The cobbler hates the Republican leader de Valera. In later life he will become a revered President; but now he is hated by the cobbler and others for having started the Civil War. All his hunched and choking fury comes to life at the sound of that execrated name.

In a rage summoned up from God knows what poisoned hell, he slides from the stool when word reaches him that the 'Broy Harriers' are coming; they're a kind of Special Branch of de Valera's police. We all know what's going to happen next. Mothers gather their children to places of safety when they see the black face of the de Valera-hater glinting like Dracula inside the window. Then, suddenly, as the Broys hove into view, the glass shatters as last and hammer come flying at them, followed in hot pursuit by the twisted cobbler himself. 'Up Dibbelera, ha!' he shouts. Like a fighting cobra erect and spitting, he comes at them with a frenzy wonderful in a half-cripple half their size. And the men of peace back off, as well they should, sensing the devil's power.

Drink is a factor in all this but despair with empty and futile lives is greater. Good housing, decent wages, better social conditions – all these will in time bring change; but none will bring the change education brings, however dimly that is seen at the time.

Our own mother is among the first to see it. 'Knowledge is no load,' she says; or, when the spartan Brothers – who will be our teachers when we eventually go to school – do their worst in corporal punishment and retribution: 'They're for yeer good; ye'll be glad of it yet!' Just stick to the books, pass the exams, and at the end of it all there'll be the reward of a fine white-collar job – below in the Corporation or 'in the civil service above in Dublin'. Not like our fathers and uncles and all our people before us, slaving it out on the docks and coalyards of Cork. Maybe it seems a small ambition now, but for Mother, for all the others like her, it was the pinnacle of her dreams. It will happen too but we don't know that now. Now, there is but faith, hope and charity – the charity of usurers and moneylenders. But to top it all, a blind but steadfast will to keep us all in place.

This marks a crucial point in the graph of a nation's progress when children of a new generation begin to think for the first time of finding a place in the sun.

From then on the slums and docks and coalyards will not condemn us to lives of hopeless poverty – and of a seething rage under the surface against the wrongs of its vindictive edicts.

It is but a small first step, yet a step just the same, on the long trek out of our dispossessed colonial past.

Our eldest brother will be our pathfinder on the way. When, at the end of his school years, years of study by candlelight and paraffin lamp, news comes that he has got himself a place in the Irish civil service, there is much rejoicing. He is our Moses, leading us out of Egypt into the Promised Land! Hot on its heels comes even better news: on her next visit to the City Hall, Mother is given the key to a new Corporation house on the south side of Cork. There is a mad splurge of borrowing and buying then, new beds and bedclothes, that white deal kitchen table and chairs of white wood to match, rolls of linoleum like liquid gold stacked up against our slum-room walls.

Bill Buckley, Mother's cousin and a carter by trade, comes along to move us over. When all our worldly goods are piled high on the dray, I am plonked up on the driver's seat beside him – the rest of them can walk. Off we go, like those share-cropping prospectors in the American midwest, hungry to inhabit our new-found world. From my perch aloft, I look back upon the place where I was born. There is a black cat in the window – one of Mad Annie's? – a sign of luck? But is the luck before us or behind? With six of us still around, there's at least a chance. Will love and life hold out long enough for us to take it?

2

'My Money and my Usances'

So we're poor and don't stop being poor because we've moved to this new house. It's the mid-1930s, a lean time everywhere, but if you really wanted to know how the other half lived at that time, Cork wouldn't have been the worst place to start.

The estate we go to has a nice name, Turner's Cross. It has a nice swanky ring to it, but that doesn't alter the fact that most people around us haven't two coppers to rub together, would count themselves lucky to have that same. So it need come as no surprise to hear that money and how to come by it is the burning issue. Any way is good if it works. Credit unions, mutual aid societies and all such benevolent enterprises are away off in the dim and distant future. For now, it's 'borrow to live and live to pay' and, if you fall by the wayside, the devil take the hindmost.

Death is our one great bonanza. Then there's money from insurance policies which are cashed in like dockets on the Grand National once the death certificate is signed. It's the only big cash most of us will ever see. All the adults are usually in on it; indeed, it's thought to be some sort of a slight on a family elder to die without all the older relatives having a policy on his or her life. Yes, of course there's grief, but grief has its consolations when the insurance man turns up among the mourners at the wake with ready cash in his pocket as an advance on the policy money which will be along in due course. Oh, death where is thy sting-a-ling-a-ling then, with crocks of gold like that springing up live under the coffin-lid! Singing and dancing were always part of the old Irish wake, but the insurance money really makes it. Small wonder that to this day I have dozens of songs by heart which I never remember learning at all – just heard them over and over again at wakes and funerals long before I was ten!

And then suddenly it stops. The dead are dead, the money dies too. But the living must live on. With the windfall gone, it's back to the same old treadmill, the same old rigmarole of pawn and loan and moneylender till the next bonanza comes around.

For all the festive seasons, Christmas, Easter, Whit Weekend and August Weekend, as well as all family events – First Communions, Confirmations, births, baptisms, weddings – moneylenders are the last resort. There's a love-hate relationship with them, as fickle as it's real.

Mother swings wildly between bouts of love and hatred, depending on who 'obliges' her or who does not in her hour of need. Seán Jennings, a furniture dealer on the Grand Parade in the middle of town, comes in for some of her fondest praise. 'Out from behind the counter he came, Mr Jennings himself,' she'll proudly tell us. 'He says I can have anything I want in his shop. "Your name is good, Mrs Murphy", he'll say; "we know you can be trusted."'

We have visions then of vanloads of furniture coming

from the Grand Parade at us. It'll be a Grand Parade in its own right, or manna from heaven, whichever you prefer. And we'll be paying for it from there to eternity!

Cavendish is the name of another furniture dealer where the same manna falls. Their van can also arrive up at the door with veneered and glossy galleons, in proof of our new-found prosperity! As they're trundled in, the neighbours peer out from behind the curtains, stunned with the wonder of it all. How can they afford such luxury? We can't, but no one thinks about that then, least of all our reckless and implacable mother, who wants only the best for her family and nothing will stop her getting it.

Father sometimes has the same problem with his benefactors who, especially at holiday-time, can offer an equally lavish service. Two of them, J. Sless and B.G. Arnold, are both Jewish, both moneylenders, who, he stoutly asserts, will give him anything he wants. 'Your word is your bond', they tell him with shameful flattery. But they always suggest that he have a trusty friend along to witness his signature – 'witness' being a nice word for 'guarantor', which is what it really means.

Pawns and pawnbrokers do a roaring trade. The 'laundry', 'Me Uncle', 'Davy Jones' Locker' are all pet-names for them; Jones was indeed the name of a string of pawnbrokers in Cork at that time.

Come Monday, and you see mothers sallying forth with big bundles under their shawls on their way to their 'Uncle' the minute the pawn-doors open. Most things are good for a 'pledge': coats, shoes, dresses, bedclothes, lamps, candlesticks, all sorts of bric-à-brac – the basic principle being that, unless the 'pledge' is redeemed, it can be subsequently sold

off. Pension-books are in a special category; pawning them is illegal both for the pawn and the borrower but needs must when the devil   drives, so they are used as collateral all the time. The idea is simple: whatever else may be left in the pawn for good, a pension-book cannot; since it is a vital part of the weekly wages, it has to be got out. So they fetch twice, three times the amount of the pension itself, a great advance at the time – but it's a once-off, while the deadweight of the weekly interest goes on forever. It's a shady business for which the 'office' is used. This is a glass cubicle to one side of the main pawn, where business is done in whispers and with only one client at a time. Oh, we all know it's 'agin' the law' but whoever took any notice of that? 'God is good', 'God's help is nearer than the door', 'Tomorrow is another day' are all hapless and helpless sedatives.

The same pawn-tickets are lyrics of abbreviation: 'St.Hng.' is 'A Suit Hanging'; 'Brn.Shs.' is 'A Pair of Brown Shoes'; 'Drs.Gn' is 'A Green Dress'. There's a great line in religious objects: 'Pr.Cndsks' is 'A Pair of Candlesticks'; 'Inf.Pg.' 'An Infant of Prague'; 'Pic.Sd.' is 'A Picture Sad' – surely the most mundane description of the Crucifixion of Christ you will ever see!   L 8 4, 5 4 7 | 920/0'muR

All this musty and dusty array of suits and shoes, coats, costumes and dresses, of bedclothes, nightclothes and dayclothes, of objects of veneration and objects of use, canteens of cutlery – the centrepiece of many a wedding present never opened, never used – bundles, packets, pots, pans, ornaments, statues, figures, frames, all these are stacked and piled high and holy in the jammed and twilight rafters of the inner pawn.

There would the noonday sun not touch and fade them, nor would the moth consume. Or so we hope, thinking of the day when they might come out again. Some few did, most did not.

In the straight-jacket of our time, their purpose is fulfilled when the pledge-money is paid. Whatever role they might have served in our lives before going in, something else, or nothing at all, would have to serve it now.

Nobody moans about it and pawnbroking is certainly not seen for what it is, legalised robbery. Rather is the pawnbroker seen as a good man, 'me Uncle', there to help when no one else can or will. Some of them even get to have an 'Uncle' look. Any more than the rest of us, I don't suppose that robbing the poor to pay the rich would have been their first choice of a job in life.

But the moneylenders are a different story. The first thing to be said about them is that they are necessary, they are a lifeline; literally we cannot live without them. But there's none of the warmth and banter of 'me Uncle' here. Small, crabbed and grabbing, they slink about in dark places with grubby books and moneybags, while the women fly to the refuge of the coal-hole in the backyard when the tocsins sound that they're on their way.

There's a regular system of African tom-toms to announce the imminent arrival of a certain 'Dickie Glue', Jewish and a usurer, but not like the 'gentlemen' of the trade, our father's friends, J. Sless and B.G. Arnold. For a clever man, Dickie makes the stupid mistake of always arriving in a taxi – an unusual sight in any place at that time – and always at the same time, which means that the children sent out to spot him can pass word along that he's there.

Small, hunched and bronchial, he's a little mouse of a man in a baggy suit and a felt hat with always half an inch of ash dangling from a cigarette-butt on his lower lip. In and out of pathways he darts, banging on doors, shouting and bawling for his repayments, with threats and curses following on his trail. The taxi noses along the road beside him as he dives in and out, like some destroying angel visiting death and vengeance on the offending doors. It's hard to see why the women are afraid of him, unless it's shame at being seen by other women who are ashamed too.

There is the fear that one day he will do what he threatens: 'Bring the van and strip the sheets and blankeys from the bed and leave the little assies freezey cold!'

One stalwart, Betsy Sullivan, has her own way of dealing with him. She has a squad of kids, her own and others, legitimate and illegitimate, though we don't use words like that for the simple reason that we don't know them. None of us ever knew Betsy's husband, who was killed in the war long, long ago.

For that, she got the widow's pension, the full whack – twenty-six and eightpence a week – but with the proviso that she would lose it instantly if she remarried. So she took the short cut, had the man but not the marriage; and for the rest of her life she had it every way, married, not married, widow's pension and lover-boy – all by the simple strategy of sticking to the strict letter of the law.

Still, with the crowd of them in there, things are always tight in Betsy's house. The menfolk in her life – her cloak of a lover and her grown-up sons – are useless when it comes to silly things like paying the rent and buying food and clothes and other such trifles. In a word, there really is only one provider – Betsy herself.

She has this great big slob of a younger boy, 'The Pope', who picks the refuse-dumps with his bosom-pal, 'Plus Fours'. When they make a killing – bottles, jamjars, all sorts of marketable junk are their trade – it's just money for the flicks on which they are world-class experts. The Pope's name comes from the time of his Confirmation, when he told the priest he was going to grow up to be so holy that he'd get the Pope's hat! Plus Fours took his from the time when he got into long trousers – his father's and miles too big and wide for him – but gradually he grew into them, which wasn't hard since he never after took them off. These are the chief watch-dogs on Friday mornings when Dickie Glue is about to arrive.

The trouble is that Dickie knows and we know that Betsy has other sons and daughters living in England and, when they come home on holidays, there are these great wild parties that go on half the night and cost the earth, for which the ever-provident Betsy pays her share. But that's Dickie Glue's money she's spending and when the sons and daughters go back and all is peace and quiet again, he'll come banging on the door for what he's due.

There will be Betsy then, stunned to insensibility by all the deaths and births and debts and burdens she's had to carry, but still up and running, on Monday mornings her arms about the bundles under her shawl, on her way to the pawn.

That'll be Monday looked after, maybe Tuesday too; but there's still Wednesday and Thursday before it's Friday when the twenty-six and eightpence pension comes in. But that's quickly gone and there's still Dickie to face.

The Pope and Plus Fours do their work well. The tom-toms send the message along. Betsy gets good warning because she lives away up near the top of the road. We trail behind the taxi until he gets to her door. Then it's a cat-and-mouse game between them, but which is cat and which is mouse is a good question. Sometimes, she'll pipe up in an incredible child's voice from behind the locked door.

'Me mother is gone out. There's no one at home.'

'Aren't you at home?' he wheezes. 'Open the door, I want to talk to her.' Then she does a vanishing trick. 'I'm no one,' she says, 'and there's no one else here.'

He won't take it. On he goes banging and wheezing till all the neighbours hear it and Betsy can't bear it any longer. Out she comes, a raging virago with pot or poker aloft, to see if she can't persuade him that discretion is the better part of valour.

'I'll do for you, I'll do for you,' she shouts, 'as true as Christ was nelt that ye crucified, I'll do for you!'

'Nelt' is nailed and 'ye' is the Jews; we're back 2,000 years to justify her pot and poker revenge. It will be some years before I begin to ask myself how poor Jewish Dickie must have felt at this lesson in Christian charity!

All this leaves out of account our own home-grown money-lender breed: sleazy customers, male and female, in fake furs and astrakhan collars; in due course they'll become the spivs and gangsters of the post-war years. At the lower end of the scale, there's the heavy brigade: 'gougers' in cloth caps and trench-coats, like the IRA of an earlier time, with God-knows-what implements of retribution to hand if their money is not repaid. That it is is due less to probity than self-interest; don't pay up and you needn't come back – and the day will come when you surely must. So eat, drink and be merry once you have them on your side. Get them offside and you'll sing for your supper from there on in.

Interest runs at usury rates – anything from twenty to fifty percent. Miss a few weeks and, with the interest com-pounded, you're into a deadly slide which sends the whole paypacket down the drain. Husbands, fathers get caught up in the galloping consumption and even the brief amnesiac of the pub can't last because the debt is still there when they get home.

The last straw is when others are dragged in – those 'witnesses' of J. Sless and B.G. Arnold who guaranteed the loan and got a few drinks for themselves in return. Then the day comes when a solicitor's letter arrives bearing tidings that more than a few drinks was involved when they signed up.

A family up the road from us hit the jackpot with a massive enterprise. It's a loan of £500 for a truck which can't be resold when the bottom falls out of the transport market. There's the scent of disaster everywhere; daily we await news of what they will do, then suddenly we wake up one morning to find that they've gone. It's the usual escape route, the *Innisfallen*, night boat to England, where they're lost and swallowed up with a million other down-and-out Irish, their life the life of the dole-queue and the penny-dinner, of night-shelters on the Thames embankment or that haven for many an Irish waif and stray, good for charity but bad for religion, the Salvation Army. But it is better than what would have happened if they had stayed at home. Then, that 'witness' who had signed up for them was their deadly enemy, expected – obliged by law – to pay up for them. This often led to dark deeds in lanes and alleys when the knives were out – and blood-money became something more than a metaphor.

The women came out of it worst of all. Frog-marched and harried for years they have been, and strange tales are told about them: one found with her head in a gas-oven; another, worse, hanging from a rafter; another still, floating down the river, her hair flowing smooth and free through the weir-grass.

24

In our house, we know well what it means – often when things are bad we hear our mother say she can't take any more and will finish it all off some way like that. She never does, but she could. And when it's dark and she's not home, we go down to the North Gate Bridge, and there, there out on the water, is a boat and men with grappling hooks pulling this thing in.

'Oh Jesus, Jesus,' we say, 'let it not be her!' They haul it in and up the steps and we crowd in around it and its face is blue and bloated – but, Jesus, Jesus, thank God it's not her; it's someone else.

Jesus help them now! As for the woman, whoever she is, it's all over for her. Dickie Glue, the furs-and-astrakhans, the trench-coat men – none of them can touch her anymore. Her eyes are shut forever upon the debts she cannot pay.

It's close on 60 years now since I laid eyes on little Jewish Dickie. A lot of water has gone under the bridge since then; a lot of blood too, including that of six million of his own kind whose angel of destruction came in the shape of the black uniform of the S.S. herding them to the horror of those gas-chambers. Our father might have been right; he used to say Dickie was one of the lucky ones: he got out in time; otherwise he might have ended up in such an oven where the fumes would have done a lot more damage to his lungs than the Wild Woodbines and the damp airs of Cork.

(A word in passing here. 'Dickie Glue', though not fictional, was not his real name. That was 'Samuel Hurwitz' – in origin German, certainly central European. I don't know if there are any of his kind still around Cork but, if there are, I would like them to know that when I name him here, I do so out of gratitude and respect: gratitude for the service he gave us at a time when no one else would; respect for the despised trade he plied among people who were themselves despised and had only him to turn to in their time of need. There were perhaps other ways in which he could have made a living; it was our good fortune that he chose this. There is only one 'now' in all our lives, the only real time there is. The past is past and will not come again; the future, if it is to come, must surely come from what we do now. Unlikely as it may seem, there was a time when he was the only stem of hope in the 'now' of our lives to see us through. In this, he was our life-line and our saviour, though at the time both he and we would surely have thought it blasphemy to say so.)

So what about the rest of us, the neighbourhood kids who followed Dickie as he trailed his asthmatic way up and down the road? Well, as the homely phrase has it, some of us 'did well'. There's a real priest and two spoilt ones amongst us, there's a journalist, a revenue expert, several singers and actors – one with an uncanny gift of mimicry, the origins of which could just about have come from a certain Betsy as she held Dickie Glue at bay long ago with that squeaky child's voice at the far side of the door. All in all, not a bad tally for a poor place, with not much to hope for in the world. We got married, had kids of our own, and went on to live happily ever after.

No pawns, no loans, no moneylenders for us; just the same thing in a different shape, old goods in brand-new wrappers: overdrafts, mortgages, never-never credits which last the lifetime they promise and in the long run end up taking as much or more than the moneylenders ever did. It's the way of the world, you take it as you find it; like it or lump it, it's not going to change.

Some did not 'do well' and ended up much as their people before them did, only the times got better and the rising tide raised all boats. A few who did not 'do well' did a lot better than the ones who did, white collars included. One was set fair to become an engine-driver like his father before him but he was fonder of football than of foot-plates and went on to become a soccer international with big money coming at him every time he changed clubs; another followed his father's footsteps as a jack-of-all-trades – and went on to run a fine car-trade of his own. None of us looks back in anger at the bad times. This may be because we've forgotten – or, like everything else in the past, only the good bits come back.

The moneylenders, those of them still around, get the occasional roasting on television. In my later RTE life, I was there when one such roasting happened, for which I shed no tears. What the TV commentators sometimes forget though – assuming, that is, that some of them ever knew! – is that the moneylenders are there because they have to be there; people with no other means cannot live without them.

The question is this: who is more to blame – they or the fat-cat pharisees who made and make their presence a necessity? Employers paying lousy wages, rulers who cream off half the same in tax, banks who rob the poor to pay the rich, property and land-speculators who look for and get crazy prices for what cannot be done without.

It is all the same sad bloody mess, 'the human condition' it's called, which persists in being so bloody inhuman much of the time. I don't suppose it will ever change. This is not to say that things have not improved – in this Ireland of ours more than most. It's been a generation or more since I saw the three brass balls dangling from a bracket outside a pawn-broker's shop; that surely means something.

Mirabile dictu, in one of those 'Davy Jones Lockers' on Shandon Street in Cork – there is a Credit Union, a good and genuine public service now gone worldwide. That one will enable the plain people of the North Side to spend their holidays on the white strands of the Canaries or Marbella – when all we could hope for was the Sunday 'Sea-Breeze Excursion' to Youghal.

So it has taken the people of my time one, maybe two, generations to come to the possibility of a better, more prov-ident, life. With that came new horizons, new ambitions, new hopes, where things like honour and decency have become part of what is theirs by right, and the black spiral of loan and usury and loan again to keep up with the usury – and maybe death by suicide at the end of it all – much of that has gone.

In our own life it stopped at last, tragically, when our father died. In other families that would have been the ultimate cat-astrophe, but remember what I said about the sudden bonanza of insurance money and you have the picture.

By now, some of us had come to sense and, unlike other such bonanzas, the money this time did not go on wild splurges of spending. Mother did what we told her: paid off the debts, shut the loan-books, started life with a clean sheet. From then on, living within what means we had, life would subtly change. Having broken the vicious circle of loan to live and live to pay, the books were balanced and the miracle of solvency achieved.

Ah, sweet mystery of life, at last I've found you – pride and joy of the aspiring working-class! Deride it not, dear friends, it gave us a sense of dignity and self-respect, things taken for granted once you have them but sorely missed when you have not.

The sad thing is that it took this last once-off bonanza on our father's life to set us free; a last tragic gesture by a man who did not live to see the many good things our later life would bring. For that I thank him, as I do for much else I did not realise at the time. There are no doubt others in my time and since – in Cork, in Ireland, in other places all over this mad but lovely world – who could tell the same story. Such is the way of our threatened life.

And such the lot of good men and women everywhere who live poor and thankless lives, so that the children of their love may one day come to know how much that love cost them.

3

'Bless me, Father'

THAT insurance money which saw us out of debt and our father out of the world wasn't the only testament to fortune he would leave. He would often say that he would die in harness, would work till he dropped, which indeed he did. There was a bit more to that than just the handy phrase: he had come through two wars, the Boer War and the 1914-18 Great War, where he had seen thousands die, horses and men – dying in harness was literally a commonplace to him. When he had had a few drinks taken, he would pull out and hold up for admiration his Social Insurance Card, stamped full week by week right up to the end. 'There's a picture,' he'd say – the simple pride of a workman never out of work. There was gratitude too – so many of his young comrades long ago had never seen such a card, never mind stamp one. Their stamps were the crosses above the graves of the 'unknown soldiers' in Flanders and the Somme or, farther afield, amongst the lush grasses of the Transvaal veldt in South Africa, so very far from the green green grass of home. 'There's a picture'

30

was both a certificate and a celebration: whatever God there was must have been on his side, that was the proof: he was back home safe and well and with a fully stamped-up card to celebrate his survival.

But back home to what? The two slum rooms in a tenement on the north side of Cork, the four flights down to the night-shift in Kilbarry when everyone else was going to bed, and four up in the morning when they were getting up; the two pounds fifteen shillings a week on Saturday when the 'picture' card was filled.

But never mind – on Sunday he was free; he could dress up and go out and be the bandbox soldier who at twenty had met and married our mother, two years younger and full of poise and beauty – and in their fashion went on to live happily ever after. From then on, the merry-go-round would never stop, except to take a new child on every so often until at last there were twelve, six of whom would live and I will be the last.

After the war, he got a job on the Great Southern Railway, a job he detested. And so he became the man I know – a porter in black corduroys and a peaked cap. The night-shift takes him away from Blarney Street before the pubs are shut and the fighting starts; but, even if he was there, he would not have had anything to do with that. Not that he wouldn't have been able; he's small but he's strong. Sometimes we ask him to show us his muscles and he rolls up his sleeves and bends his arms and up they come up in round hard little footballs.

Only once ever did we hear of him being in a fight. That was in Currie's pub across the road where he was with our Uncle Johnny, Mother's brother – the one who lost a leg with the Munster Fusiliers in the Dardanelles. One night, Johnny is leaning forward to take his pint from

the counter when one of his crutches slips and he acci-
dentally knocks the drink from the hand of the man beside
him. The man gets angry and shoves him and gets as far
as the word 'fucking cripple' when Father lets fly and
sends him out through the plate-glass window.

That's the only time we hear about him being in a fight.
He's just not that sort of man.

Well, what sort of man is he then?

First off, he is not the man our mother says she married all
those years ago. That was her soldier boy, all gilt and polish,
like the ones in the toy boxes at Christmas. The day she married him, he was decked out in the regimental finery of the
Dublin Fusiliers, one of the Irish regiments in the British
Army: red tunic trimmed with gold, glengarry cap, gleaming
black boots and – the crowning glory – razor-creased black
trousers with a red pinstripe down the outer seam. His best
man was the same, but pride and glory were the six com-
rades-in-arms with swords aloft in a celebration arch for the
bride and groom as they came down the North Cathedral
steps. It was, she would say, the proudest moment in her life:
the gleaming swords, the red tunics and burnished boots, the
pinstripe on the trousers-seam – it was a heaven-sent dream
to the eighteen-year-old Cinderella from the slums of the
North Side.

There is a picture of her from that time, all mist and
dignity, her long black hair braided in three rolls above her
forehead and her eyes looking fixed upon some future perfection that would surely come.

Shortly after that, he left her and went off to the first of
his wars against the Boers in South Africa. His Regimental
Book attests that he was 5 feet 4 inches tall, had a healthy

complexion, grey eyes and brown hair – all physical features one might think would not change much in the space of a few years. But when she next saw him, she had no idea who he was. The war was over and the regimental colours were being trooped in a march up through Patrick Street and along the Grand Parade.

'Christ, he's burnt copper', her own mother standing beside her exclaimed when the sun-tanned soldier-boy was pointed out to her in the line.

Shortly after, he was gone again – this time to Egypt, the Sudan and the islands of the Mediterranean – Gibraltar, Malta, Cyprus, Crete. By then, the distance between him and the lanes and alleyways of Cork had grown; but, alas, his teenage sweetheart would still have a lot more celibate living to do before his soldier-days were done.

That Regimental Book also tells me something else I hardly need to be told: that his father's name was William, that being the reason I am William too. I am in fact the second William; the first died in infancy before I was born. Make no mistake, the name 'William Murphy' was going to be remembered alright!

That older William was, we're told, a remarkable man. A person of dignity, we are assured, of body, of mind, of spirit – all features which I am exhorted to inherit when my time comes. When he comes home on pay-nights with a few drinks on board, Father will stand me before him and tell me my name is William Murphy, 'after your grandfather'. Then he'll make me promise that I'll be like him in all respects when I grow up. He even instructs me in how I must make the promise: I must say 'I'll try'. The reward for this singular feat of fidelity is a penny. It is an early lesson in the psychology of acquiescence.

William the elder was tall, dark and handsome, all

features in which I, his grandson namesake, must have much disappointed him.

It was, Mother would tell us, a mighty sight to see that William Murphy with his bosom friend, Hugh Miller, walking into town together on Sunday morning: two 'Gentlemen of Verona' set in the midst of their hapless, penny-farthing life. To add to their distinction, Hugh Miller was a Scot and wore a kilt – not, I suspect, the rugby-and-fashion nonsense of later times but part of a real Scotsman's walking-out dress. Both of them had been British army-men and the ramrod disciplines remained. I do not know who led who in their mutual admiration society but what is a fact is that Hugh Miller's son married William Murphy's daughter – the 'Auntie Nonie' I will come to know in later years; a marriage which produced a new dynasty of Murphy-Millers, all tall, dark and handsome – and none more so that that godfather of mine, Tygeen, cavalry-man in the Great War. He and Father would in time become great friends; and, if I am seeking now for a picture of army-men in their prime in those years, all I have to do is remember the pair of them stepping it out behind the hearse at Auntie Nonie's funeral, certainly the best example of square-bashed military discipline I have ever seen.

There is another side to this grandfather William Murphy: what we may call his intellectual side. For among his singular array of attributes, none was rarer than his skill with figures. In hushed and reverent silence, we would be told, 'That man could tell how many times the clock ticked in a year!'

To us, it is a truly stunning achievement: to follow tick by tick every second of the clock of Shandon, sleeping or waking to be able to count and remember every one of them! But such are the benefits of a liberal education and such the daring of precocious youth that one day when I am ten and the mysteries of the multiplication table have begun to unfold themselves, I sit up at the kitchen table and work it out: 60 x 60 x 24 x 365. And there, lo and behold, is the magic figure: 31,536,000!

Father's mouth opens in awe and his eyes come alive with pride. 'By Christ,' he says, 'I made no mistake in calling you "William" after him alright!'

About his mother we hear little. Anything we do hear comes from others, not from him. One event in their life together suggests a rough relationship: this was when she stripped him of his clothes after he had been in some scrape and tied him to the leg of the bed; but he promptly untied himself the minute her back was turned to make his escape, his legs stuck in the sleeves of her cardigan with twine about the waist. She appears in that Regimental Book of his as 'Eliza Flynn', the only time I will ever see her name. Unlike his father, about whom he can hardly speak without weeping, she is a pale, forgotten shade who, it seems, unlike the rest of her tough breed could not take the strains of life in that starved and sacrificial time. There were no nice words like 'mentally disabled' or 'psychiatric' in those days; so we are bluntly told that she ended her days in the 'madhouse' (if you wanted to be really grand, the 'lunatic asylum'). It's still there, its grey ghostly towers and spires draped above the banks of my own lovely Lee. It has long since ceased to be a hospital, but the structure is still magnificent. All I hope is that in the long summer nights when 'the maid and her lover the wild daisies press', or when its opulent new clientele walk about the landscaped grounds, they will not be too troubled by the ghosts of Christmas past, especially Eliza Flynn, whose fiery particle of a son spoke so long and lovingly about that William Murphy who was once her man, but alas never about her.

Father's night-shift on the railway in Kilbarry is a lonely job, his only company being the cattle and goods trains which are being 'shunted' all night long. To me it sounds like a curse-word, maybe to the men who do it it's a curse-word too. But at least he's alone there; he has a little corrugated hut, his 'canteen' he calls it, where he can come and go as he pleases.

When the shift is over, he comes home in the early hours and makes more tea with lots of sugar in it; it's a brief moment when things are right. Then, it's bed and the sleep of the just – let the rest of the world go by. We're gone off to school, the house is quiet, the din and clamour of Goulnaspurra, with the horses and carts trundling by and the men and women shouting at each other, mean nothing to him. Like that Prince Hamlet I will come to know about in later times, my railway-porter father, though bounded in a nutshell, for those brief hours is king of infinite space. It is a kingdom and a reign that will not last.

At last Mother's dream comes true: we get this new Corporation house and Kilbarry is too far for him to walk. That's when he is transferred to the goods yard of the station in Glanmire, a short distance from home but a million miles from the peace and quiet of Kilbarry. From the very first, he hates the place and all to do with it; above all, he hates the pettiness of the people with power over him; worse still the ones who put on arselick smiles to please them. One small example will suffice. It's an overcoat, part of the winter uniform given to all the porters; but it has a certain status attached, so it must be asked for as a favour from the inspector. This is a big bully with a braided cap and a stubby pipe between his teeth, like the bit in a horse's mouth. For good measure, his name is Power, a name he much relishes. Father cannot bring himself to ask for something which he should have by right, so the overcoat does not come and he must face the winter without it. This night it comes bitterly cold and we see him cutting circles out of the *Evening Echo* through which he can shove his head to make an undervest of several layers of paper beneath his shirt.

Is there something deeper here than his hatred of power and the abuse of it? A sense of dignity and the loss of dignity, of the rape and plunder of a decent man's right by someone whom the blind hand of fate has placed in authority above him? It will be years before I catch the authentic tone of our father's attitude in all this. It is from 200 years before and 100 miles away – in the verses of the eighteenth-century Kerry poet, Aogán Ó Rathaille (translated by Frank O'Connor), forced to beg favours from a new and foreign master after his own native patrons have been put down.

> That my old bitter heart was pierced in this black doom,
> That foreign devils have made our land a tomb,
> That the sun that was Munster's glory has gone down
> Has made me a beggar before you, Valentine Brown ...
>
> Garnish away in the west with its master banned,
> Hamburg the refuge of him who has lost his land,
> An old grey eye, weeping for lost renown,
> Has made a beggar before you, Valentine Brown.

So who are his patrons then, the ones he looks up to with respect? Certainly, they are nowhere near him now; they go back to his army days, away back to the Boer War in fact, when briefly, for one glorious day, he became a soldier of note. This was during a Dublin Fusiliers parade in Pretoria in which he 'took the stick' – a token white baton awarded to the smartest soldier in the regiment. This earned him the further award of being made batman to the one of the colonels, Lord Lonsdale, friend and coeval of the Churchills, Haldane, Julian Amery – 'the captains and the kings' of the British colonial elite. It was heady stuff for a wild Irish boy out on his first foray away from the slums and lanes of Cork.

Years later, when his glory-days are long since over and times are bad, his one good suit and pair of shoes will go off to the pawn on Monday morning – to keep the home-fires burning for the coming week. When they are redeemed the following Friday, he will set about them with iron and steam-cloth, while the shoes, already perfect to my eyes, will be tinted with marker ink to brink up their ruby sheen and then polished until there's a glint of light from them. By Sunday, when he's dressed up, with the starched shirt and brown 'couteau' hat, he's the picture of perfection. If there was a 'stick' going in Cork, he'd have won it hands down all the time.

We are all proud of him and love to be seen with him as he goes down town to meet his friends and walk with them along the length of the Grand Parade and Patrick Street. It's a brief return to old glories – brief because by Monday the suit and shoes are bundled away again, to moulder in the mothballs of 'Davy Jones' Locker' until the next Friday.

That instinct for perfections in our father can take on less personal forms. Once, through some financial wizardry of our mother's, we are down for a week's holiday in a little shack in Crosshaven at the mouth of the harbour, and he's left at home alone to look after himself. When we come back on Sunday night, the house is gleaming: the floorboards scrubbed white, the walls and ceilings washed down, the gardens trimmed and barbered like some corner of Titania's Palace.

That 0075 Private Kennedy Murphy, out from the town of Cork in the South of Ireland to fight the Boers, probably never heard of those 'masters' of British colonial Africa until he got there – Cecil Rhodes, Lord Roberts, Kitchener of Khartoum, General Sir Redvers Buller – those heroes of song and story whose praises he will sing for the rest of his life. That colonial world of Kipling and the Gods of Empire will be for him a world of chivalry and regimental loyalty – and the mad and mindless regimental ballads that go with it:

> 'They're as brave, they're as bold, as the armoured knights of
>   old,
> Hats off to them we must exclaim.
> For in our darkest hour of need, 'twas they helped us to suc
>   ceed
> For the honour of old England's name.'

This particular generation of Irishry – before the liberation movements of the first years of the new century – were sodden ripe for exploitation, steeped as they were in that tradition of Empire and starved for centuries of any sense of a national identity of their own. Blessedly, they will be the last victims of such blind and craven apostasy. Their Empire allegiance is cunningly instilled as loyalty to faith and fatherland; whose faith and whose fatherland, they are too brainwashed to ask. The 'Dubs', as they're known, have a proud and honoured name which it is the duty of the men of their time to uphold. For in times past hadn't they sung of them in the far-off Crimea:

Devils they, not mortal men, the Russian general swore,
As we tore them off the Alma Heights in September '54.

It is a sentiment which would soon have its Boer War
equivalent:

Bravely fought upon the Glencoe Heights,
Put five thousand crafty Boers to flight,
It was a grand, a glorious sight –
Bravo, the Dublin Fusiliers!

All this would become fused in our father's mind with
the adventures of war and the stimulus of new places; and,
though in other respects a man of sceptical mind, he will
never recover from that primal indoctrination. Like the good
player who will always cherish the team he played with as a
young man, he will love the 'Dubs' to his dying day and can
barely contain himself when singing their fatuous and jingoistic anthems:

We drink tonight because we are so jolly,
We drink tonight to Buller, White and Colley,
Somebody gave the toast to every man's delight:
'Here's to old Buller, and long may he reign' –
And that's why we drink tonight.

It was in this Buller's time that an event happened which
would become one of the great talking points of Father's life.
This was to do with a Boer ambush of a British armoured
train in which their officer-in-charge, one Julian Amery, was
badly wounded. The convoy would have been massacred
but for the courage and decisiveness of a young journalist
reporting the war for his newspaper back in London who
happened to be accompanying his friend Amery and
promptly took command when he was wounded. It so

happened that this young man had been the dinner-guest of Lord Lonsdale the night before; Father actually served him at table. The story made headlines in all the South African and English papers the following day and Father would proudly tell how he had picked up the *Capetown News* to find on the front page the picture of the young hero who had saved the day: Winston Churchill.

So the Boer War finished and that should have been that. But soon he was off again. Those were the years in North Africa and the Mediterranean, when the streets of Malta's Valetta and Crete's Heraklion became as familiar as the well-known streets of Cork which must sometimes have faded from his mind.

Then, Bismarck came along, with the legacy of a new united Germany, big and strong enough to take on the world's powers. So he's off again – this time to fight the 'Huns', not the Boers. He's into his mid-thirties by now and must have had his fill of wars; what's more, he has a wife and they have a family. But the 'Dubs' are in his blood and enlistment is more a matter of pride than of duty. So away he goes on another merry-go-round, this time to the mud and trenches of Flanders and No-Man's-Land. But the regimental rhymers are active as always in urging them on:

> They may build their ships, my lads,
> Think they know the game,
> But they can't build the boys of the bulldog breed
> That made old England's name.

By now, though, some dawning awareness of the plunder of gullible loyalties will make him add an acidulous reprise:

> Send out your brother, your sweetheart or your mother –
> But for Christ-sake don't send me!

Yet for all its death and slaughter, the mud and the swamps and the squalor, it is still possible for him to dream of the future for which they think they are fighting: 'a land fit for heroes to live in', which British Prime Minister Lloyd George so cunningly holds out. What matter if it will turn out – for them in Ireland, 'the first colony of Empire', it certainly turns out – to be the same slums and debtors and love-on-the-dole; if the children who are lucky get to manhood, and those who are not are luckier still because they avoid what coming to manhood means; if the young and lovely grow old and ugly before their time; and if spirited and comely girls become battered and gnarled harridans fighting their menfolk for the bread and board that are supposed to be their due?

What matter about all that in the trenches of the Somme, for even in the midst of all the death and maiming, hope springs eternal in the human beast and is a dim rushlight to relieve the horror of their living days.

Anyway, one day it is all over, Father is demobbed and comes back to a quiet life in the Civvy Street of Cork. It's a very different Civvy Street from the one he left. That Regimental Book has him signing out on 24 March 1919 – twenty years to the day after he had signed in. That very year would see the meteoric rise of a new political party in Ireland – Arthur Griffith's Sinn Féin, which wiped out the constitutional party of John Redmond in a landslide electoral victory.

The blood-sacrifice of the Insurrection of 1916, the leaders of which were executed, had swept aside the ethic of Empire; the era of polite politics was over, the physical force men would make the running from now on. Yeats, an unlikely balladeer, puts it well:

O but we talked at large before
The sixteen men were shot,
But who can talk of give and take,
What should be and what not
While those dead men are loitering there
To stir the boiling pot?

In the years that followed, the heroes of song and story will no longer be the heroes of the Somme and Ypres but the men of the flying columns of the IRA who, at places like Kilmichael and Crossbarry, carried out small strategic ambushes aimed at paralysing the occupying forces – the forerunner of all guerrilla wars. Soon, the red tunic of the Dublin Fusiliers is seen in the streets no more, the very name of the Irish regiments in the British Army dare scarcely be mentioned. And with them perishes the whole colonial ethic, its wars seen now for what they were: meaningless fights in another nation's interests, for which Father and his like were cannon-fodder – and all for the pension of fifteen shillings a week if you lived or twenty-six and eightpence if you died, a fine memento for the housefuls of orphans left behind.

It's all over now, for Father and the rest of them, the 'Dubs', the 'Munsters', the 'Connaught Rangers', the 'Leinster Rifles'; they can all hang up their boots and their rifles. There will be no more foreign wars for them to fight in anymore.

So he becomes that man in black corduroys and a peaked cap I come to know, a railway porter in Kilbarry and the goods yard of Cork. Not much, but better than selling card-matches outside theatres, like many another who came back to that 'land fit for heroes'. It is in this later phase, the last fifteen years, that father comes into our lives. He is a strange mixture of a man by now, much at odds with the political climate of this new Ireland, with its public celebration of the deeds of the freedom-fighters and no celebration at all of the deeds of men like him; with its fire-and-brimstone church missions to shrive and save us from eternal damnation; with its native Irish language which his children will come to learn at school, though no one in his or our mother's family has spoken it for generations. Not that he would have been against such things if he had the slightest chance to know them. But education for him was in a wholly foreign and a strictly English mode, especially the poetry of Empire, Kipling above all and, with him, the most flagrantly Blimpish of his verse. 'Gunga Din' is a great favourite, he never seems to tire of it:

> Now in Injia's sunny clime,
> Where I used to spend my time
> A-servin' of 'er Majesty the Queen,
> Of all them blackfaced crew
> The finest man I knew
> Was our regimental bhisti, Gunga Din ...

> Yes, Din! Din! Din!
> You Lazarushian-leather, Gunga Din!
> Though I've belted you and flayed you,
> By the livin' Gawd that made you,
> You're a better man than I am, Gunga Din!

The image of the black-faced water-carrier in service, if not in slavery, to the cork-helmeted – sometimes cork-brained! – captains of Empire, and that at a time when the idea of workers' rights had taken root in the world at large, was more than some of us could take.

Yet our father, who surely saw many such slave-figures in his own childhood – to say nothing of later times in the Sudan, Egypt and the Transvaal – seemed quite at home with the Kipling line. It was as simple as this: Her Majesty the Queen and her agents, the spin-doctors of that time, could think, say or do no wrong. This was all the more surprising in a man who would burn with rage at the injustice of someone lowly, like himself, being put upon by someone a notch or two above, like that Inspector Power of his goods yard days.

But for a man who had left school when he was ten, he has one attribute which is quite remarkable: his handwriting. A letter in his hand is a very classic in calligraphy. I remember one in particular: It begins – 'Sire' – and is addressed to 'His Majesty King George V'. It has something to do with his pension – for his four years in the trenches, he has the princely sum of fifteen shillings a week; add ten more to that for the Boer War. The letter is one thing, the reply when it comes is another. It's from the Ministry of Pensions, it's on an octavo sheet, it's typewritten, and it's signed by some anonymous official who makes himself doubly anonymous by a scrawl at the end which none of us can make out. What it says is a curt 'No' to whatever it was that he was petitioning his 'Sire' for. There's ne'er a mention of King George at all.

That may have been one of the days when he feels that the honour and chivalry he so prized in the 'Dubs' are dead; and that the King and Country he was willing to fight and die for might be worth a sight less than the twenty-five bob a week they were willing to give him!

In other ways, though, and bearing in mind that he never did have any real schooling, he can, upon occasion, be quite the scholar. He comes to life suddenly when he hears one of us boys reciting a verse of poetry for our homework; what seems a drudge and a deadweight to us is a delight to him; he makes us say it over and over again until he has it by heart. The rhythmic verses of Tennyson and Wordsworth make a special appeal, also the set-pieces of Shakespeare – 'The quality of mercy is not strained', 'Tomorrow, and tomorrow, and tomorrow'. He says queer things like 'they're holy' and 'they lift the spirit' – things that make no sense at all to us but he shuts his eyes and seems to drink them in. They are delayed-action shots of some magic thing which will come out in us later on.

In this he is our teacher and our guide, leading us by strange and wayward steps towards the kind of men and women we will be. Speaking for myself, if there is anything of that feeling and that spirit in me, anything of its insights and understanding and sense of our imperilled human condition, it is in no small measure due to the lifelines he flung to us with those early shafts of wisdom.

So, he is a dreamer, an inspirer, a soul-maker – but one thing he is not is a religious man. There are brief spells when the annual Mission comes round and all the men troop down to church for the fire-and-brimstone sermons of the Redemptorists, great hell-raising stuff meant to put the fear of God in them, which it does too for a time. But then after a while, the echoes die down and – for him at least – it's back to the same old theme: 'The men who lived through Flanders and the Somme know what hell is – and they don't need any smock-frocked priest to tell them!' I don't know if this is in his mind when the church-bells ring for Benediction on Sunday nights and he chants out in time with them: 'Bring on your tainted money!' Mother flies into a rage with him then and tells him to 'stop, you're scandalising the children'. Which he might very well be, if we knew for a moment what 'scandalise' meant. More to the point in our hand-to-mouth life is that it's Sunday, his one day off, and now it's over, and he hands up to her whatever few shillings he has left from his session in Dinny Byrne's. For tonight we'll merry-merry be, tomorrow we'll be sober! It's back to the grindstone then and, Benediction-bells or no bells, there will be no more money, tainted or otherwise, from then until the end of that week.

I have just about begun to have some inkling of what all this is about – that my father does not have a 'big' job like some of those bosses of his, that there is no money and not much of anything else – but I have not yet made the connection between that and his own bleak sense of failure: the smartest of the bandbox Fusiliers who had 'taken the stick' in Africa and is now stomping about in thick corduroys pulling a loaded bogey in the goods yard, like some black caterpillar trawling his weight behind him. He most of all does not want me to see him like this – fearing, as well he might, that it will kill the dream for better things which he has been building up.

But luckily, before that happens, something else does which changes the whole picture of our lives.

This is the Cork Corporation Scholarship Exam in which I take first place. Modesty bedamned: it is one hell of an achievement for a boy from a school in the slums and lanes. It is three in the afternoon of the day the results come out when I arrive in the goods yard to tell him the news. He is unloading sacks of sugar from a wagon onto his bogey when he sees me. Instantly, he drops the bogey and beckons me over to the corrugated canteen where there is no one else about just then. When I tell him, he says nothing but walks away from me over to the stove in the corner where he stands warming his hands for what seems a very long time. I know the silence means something but I do not know what it is. When he turns back, his eyes are red. I think this is the smoke but then I see the tears and know it is not. He tries to say something but the words will not come. He just stands there with his hands on my shoulders and looks and looks at me.

I think I know now what he is trying to say. It is his father's name – 'William Murphy'.

The scholarship is worth 80 pounds, a lot of money then. When the instalments are paid, as they will be every Christmas and Easter for the four years of secondary school, I will be briefly an opulent young man. What my father gives me is sixpence. Small, by comparison, though I have to say it's the most money anyone has given me up to then. But to me it is more than sixpence. It is the same as the thing he has for his father, that other William Murphy, whenever he speaks of him. It is his heart.

All this time, he has the most racking cough, legacy of the trenches – by no means helped by the wretched Woodbines, 'coffin-nails' they're called, which he smokes all the time. He seems to be always cold. He puts it down to the years in Africa and the Mediterranean – but how could it be that when it happened so long, long ago?

At last, it gets so bad that the doctor is called. He's the British Army Panel Doctor, so he does not have to be paid; otherwise he would not be called.

After a brief examination, he tells us our father is exhausted and will have to stop work. How easily the rich can solve the problems of the poor! So now, small as it is,

48

the weekly paypacket is gone, with nothing in its place but ten shillings a week National Health; that and the St Vincent de Paul.

It all comes together one of those days when he's at home sick. He daren't show his face outside because the National Health will be stopped if he's seen. So it becomes Mother's task to bring him his daily Woodbines. By now, they're the habit of a lifetime; he cannot give them up. But so is eating, which we cannot give up. The packet costs twopence which is also the price of a loaf of bread. Mother, torn between loyalties, must make the choice. When she comes home, he is sitting at the window, an old coal-sack over his knees. She hands him the packet and he takes it. There is a look of shame and failure in his eyes. Not a word passes between them.

So, my beloved parents, shall the meek not inherit the earth.

That autumn of my scholarship will be the last autumn of his life. He gets quieter; there is a lot less talk of old wars and the boys of the old brigade. For the first time in the years since I have come to know him, he just sits there, saying nothing. I have understood little of his talk but I do not understand this at all. He seems to be listening, as if to some voice or message which he cannot quite hear. I am thirteen and do not yet know about the thin line between life and death, and the silence without words that is in between.

One night around that time he brings home with him one of his soldier mates, a relative of our mother's, a brash and boastful ould fellow who was with the Irish Guards in the war, cream of the Irish regiments – and he's not letting any of us forget it! Soon, with the drink stirring, he is at full throttle, bawling away for all he's worth the anthem of the Irish Guards, 'Fogaballa is the War-Cry of the Gael' ('Fogaballa' from the Irish *Fág an Bealach*, clear the way). It's a stupid bloody song, full of self-praise, but when it comes to the chorus, which we happen to know, we're all expected to join in.

Dutifully, we do – at least it'll shout the ould bugger down! But Father does not. He sits there, silent and withdrawn in this new mode of his, his eyes fixed and staring in front of him at something we cannot see.

When it's finished, he makes no attempt to match it with one of his own war-songs, 'Athenry' or 'Bravo, the Dublin Fusiliers'; instead, he comes out with some verses by his great favourite, Kipling:

> If you can talk with crowds and keep your virtue,
>   Or walk with Kings – nor lose the common touch,
> If neither foes nor loving friends can hurt you,
>   If all men count with you, but none too much;
> If you can fill the unforgiving minute
>   With sixty seconds' worth of distance run,
> Yours is the Earth and everything that's in it,
>   And – which is more – you'll be a Man, my son!

Armistice Day, 11 November – the day the war ended in 1918 – is commemorated each year on the Sunday nearest the date. In preparation for it, my father takes out his regimental medals – the Mons Star, the Ypres Cross, the Medal for Long Service and Good Conduct, the one for Honour and Bravery; he polishes them and, with the Flanders poppy, goes out with the other old soldiers to take his place. When it's over, he takes them off and puts them back in their wooden box until the next year's parade comes around. For him, there will not be a next year's parade; he will not take them out again. The cough gets worse, the fool of a Panel Doctor, who has been feeding him war-talk when he might have been giving him some medicine, diagnoses bronchitis when even a child can see it's worse. And then he sends him off to hospital. It's the last humiliation, for the hospital is the County Home, 'The Union', with all that word implies. By day, the 'paupers' – there's no mincing of words in those days – lumber about the wards in great hob-nailed boots, their thick grey homespuns the mark and brand of destitution.

At night, when the lights go out, an old man in the bed beside him jabbers in senile decay into the small hours. It is not an end that the boy who had 'taken the stick' with 'The Dubs' in Africa had ever thought would come.

On New Year's Eve, my three older brothers go to see him. They bring him half a dozen Guinness to help pass the time. When they're finished, they ask him what to do with the empties. He says nothing but jumps out of bed, opens the window and sends them flying into the cobbled yard below. There is a glasshouse there where by day the 'paupers' do occupational work. The missiles go shattering through the glass roof, waking the whole house. The following day, he is discharged, his 'bronchitis' suddenly and miraculously cured.

I sometimes think about that New Year's Eve, the last our father will ever see on earth. Has he finally come to realise that he has not long to go? That crashing glass in a poorhouse yard – what is it saying? That they will not take this son of fire alive? It is his last fling; he will not come again.

He had not been to Mass for a long time, had long ago given up Confession, Communion and all that; so, in the the-ology of his time, he is a lost soul, dead to God and the church; yet I pray for him now all the time, knowing that a good man is good despite those things, and that his rage at dying was the rage in Dylan Thomas' – at being robbed of a life he had once loved and of a gift he would have made more of if only he had been given half a chance:

> And you, my father, there on the sad height,
> Curse, bless, me now with your fierce tears, I pray.
> Do not go gentle into that good night.
> Rage, rage against the dying of the light.

We buried him in the new cemetery at Douglas, out on the edge of town. He is with the other soldiers there; *that* he would have liked. There is a green hill above the place with a copse of beech on top, and in the evening great flocks of birds gather to make a fine, bosky sound.

It is a far cry from the poppy-fields of Flanders and farther still from the broad veldt of the Transvaal, in any of which places he might have left his bones. There is a stone above his grave with nothing on it but his name. If it were bigger and we had known it, we might have added a line from Siegfried Sassoon: 'Look up, and swear by the slain of Flanders that you will not forget.'

I do not think we will.

4

SEX IN A DAMP CLIMATE

MOTHER is 45 when she feels the first stirrings of what will become me. Father is two years older. I am the twelfth intruder upon their life. It is, I reasonably conclude, a life which must know a lot about sex. Yet that dread word is never spoken. The idea of our father and mother having anything remotely to do with it would be abhorrent.

This is so not only with us; it is the great taboo with everyone around us. This may have its roots somewhere in our rural past: in the minute land-divisions, steadily declining from age to age as new families came along and the same parcels of land had to be divided up; or in the staple diet of potatoes and milk, high on protein and good for body-building – until the failure of the potato-crop and the catastrophic Famine that followed. After that, for those who wanted some sort of a life, it was the emigrant ship to the new world – sometimes, alas, the 'coffin-ship'; for those who stayed, a bleak and loveless peasant life – the life of a serf or slave to all intents and purposes, except for the eldest male, who got the family land. There would be no sex, no marrying, no anything at all for anyone else.

But that's before our time. Still, habits long forming long remain. The free and fecund life of love in a warm climate are certainly not for us. But the thrust is there; active or inactive it goes on, and a major local trade develops – in illicit sex, frustrated sex, started-but-not-finished sex, half, three-quarters and nine-tenths sex; and when the last tenth can't wait, the babies come.

It is easy to blame this on our inbred Catholic past, for that is where the ground-rules are laid down. The Great Giver of the Commandments may have decreed that there are but two: love God and love thy neighbour. But for us there are another two which take more menacing precedence, the Sixth and Ninth in our school Catechism: 'thou shalt not commit adultery'; 'thou shalt not covet thy neighbour's wife'. All else is secondary to those Tablets of Stone.

So the emphasis in our growing lives is on chastity and how to keep it; on the virtue of holy purity, which will ensure a state of grace and get us into heaven; on avoiding, under pain of eternal damnation, those wildly seductive and ever-present 'occasions of sin'. There are special prayers and devotions to help us; rarely a day passes when we are not enjoined to avail of them. The blackest pits of hell are reserved for those who offend. To be fair, few do; this may be due as much to habit and the prevailing custom as to any moral reason. But it is also owing to a widespread awareness of the dire consequences that follow if the rules are broken and things go wrong.

The consequences are immeasurably worse for the girl. Though sex-talk is banned, we have the essentials from the bush-telegraph, the first and most important of which is that it is the girl who carries the baby. The thrust has to be very unstoppable to let this happen. A firebrand of vengeance may indeed descend upon the boy who could not stop – but it is ten times worse upon the girl who could not stop him.

Fathers storm out of the house in a rage and go off down to the pub to drown the shame and disgrace of it. They come back roaring that 'the hoor has to be got out of here'; that he'll 'get the bastard who did this'. Distraught mothers connive at a hasty marriage; failing that, at a sudden mysterious vanishing to England; failing that again, that 'she's gone to help her aunt with the children'; finally, when the evidence is becoming so obvious that it cannot be ignored, that she's simply 'gone away'. 'Away' means 'The Good Shepherd Convent', where, to help pay her keep, the errant one does laundry work for the upper classes. It is where many a milk-and-honey love-tryst will end.

For the male offender – the 'bastard', 'hoor-master', 'fornicator' – there is a wide and varied range of choice: he can marry the girl and go on to live happily ever after – some do and, strangely, it sometimes works; he can slip away in the night on the *Innisfallen* and never be heard of again; or he can stick it out and face the music, including the night of the long knives.

This will come in some dark alleyway when he least expects it, when he thinks the whole thing is over and long forgotten: coming home from a night in the Arcadia Ballroom where the trouble started in the first place; worse still, coming home from the pub on a Saturday night when he's foot-loose and fancy-free, with all his cares behind him. Then suddenly he's caught up in a maelstrom of boots, cudgels and sticks – worse still, the flash of razor-blades and knives. His brief moment of rapture will then give him most unrapturous things to remember. 'Ah, sweet mystery of life, at last I've found you': find it he did indeed and lived to regret it. So endeth the story of 'love's old sweet song'.

Pray do not make the mistake, as many do, of thinking that this is only in 'holy Ireland'. It is in holy, and unholy, everywhere. It is in Lorca's torrid *House of Bernarda Alba* where the jaunty lover, Pepe El Romano, gallops off on his stallion, having planted his illicit seed in one of her daughters. And the women foregather, like the witches in *Macbeth*, to devise a dire retribution. For the girl, it will be 'coals of fire upon the place where she sinned.' It is in the white palatial mansions of Tennessee Williams' *Deep South* where her brave young lover has taken 'Heavenly', the cotton-baron's daughter, his 'Sweet Bird of Youth', when she's virgin-ripe – and he's startled by the glinting of knives when he comes to seek her a second time. It's in that holy of holies, the Cathedral of Nôtre Dame in Paris, where the good and righteous Canon Fulbert hears of the rape of his student niece, the lovely Héloïse, by her scholar-teacher Abelard and sets his thugs upon him to inflict the castrate marks that will distinguish his once-male voice forever in the august halls of the Sorbonne.

Nor should it be thought that in a male-dominated world it is always the male who leads and the female who is led on. Let it be clearly said that in no case do the offended innocents show any but an ardent desire to be deflowered. No more than nature's flower denies the moth or the scented musk the bee, neither do they reject the honeyed mouths that tell them they are loved.

And so it is with us. Be not judgmental then of our Irish ways; in such matters we are no different from anyone else on earth. We see the light of love in each other's eyes and we are less than human if we do not respond to it. There are, however, differences in kind which our climate and our history have made for us.

Some of these do indeed have a religious base but, religion or no religion, for the most part they are with us from our mother's womb. From that same mother and that same father who, as the facts amply show, had a full sexual life of their own; but as time went on they became rightly fearful of what such a life might mean for their innocent offspring if they got the taste of it too soon.

What is a fact is that the priests did have us in a bit of a knot about all this. This includes nuns and brothers, the whole religious/educational establishment in fact, to which our parents ceded responsibility for our sexual development – repression might be nearer the mark. The Sixth and Ninth Commandments were away on top of the agenda, with the sex-sermon at the annual Mission a guaranteed sell-out. Whether we were there to learn about sex or to learn how to avoid it is a good question. One thing is certain: it had to be a fairly burning issue in everyone's life to gain such a rapt audience. You can hear a pin drop in the church when the preacher gets to the core of it: those woodbined nooks in the hedgerows out beyond 'The Black Ash' where the devil's spore is in the air, mixed with the scent of hawthorn and the new-mown hay; the double-seats in The Savoy and Pavilion where the conniving dark sets probing hands in search of Satan's work; worst of all – because sex and money are conjoined – the back seat of the parked car on the lonely road where there is neither eye nor mind to stay the fiend; and mortal lips and mortal hands go straight in quest of mortal sin.

The 'do's and 'don't's, the warning caveats and rules, the commandments of God and the precepts of the Church – all these are laid out in grim array before us. At least we cannot say we have not been warned. But there will still be miscreants, and there are sterner measures for them.

Our parish priest has entered the hall of fame with a verse which is on all our lips:

Canon Cunnane is a holy man,
He goes to Mass on Sunday
And prays to God to give him the grace
To beat the boys on Monday.

Beating the boys is not his sole pastoral work. Nor does it confine itself to Monday. All the other days of the week when dusk comes down, he puts on his black coat and hat and with a stout blackthorn goes off on his nightly prowl. Those woodbined nooks drowsed with the scent of hawthorn and the new-mown hay are an early target. They are beds of iniquity and the devil's lair; by instinct, if not by experience, he knows it. Soft as a cat he approaches until the tell-tale yelps and giggles from behind the bushes betray them. With unerring aim, he prods at them and hauls them out; it is the hand of God snatching them from the jaws of hell. If the jaws of hell could see what he sees then, they would snap tight with fright – or admiration! There is much frantic buttoning and zipping as the errant pair come forth, like Adam and Eve caught in the act in the Garden. The good man knows then that he is right, that he is about God's work. And there's still more work to do in the woodbine-scented nooks and crannies to come.

The Mardyke is a long and elegant vista of beech-trees beside the river Lee, heavy with leaf on summer nights. It is a place where lovers go to talk the endless nothings young lovers talk while gathering their strength – or weakness – to do more positive things. It can be strenuous work, so it is nice to lean against the trees while at it. But, this is Satan country and the shady beech and gathering dusk are great connivers, certain occasions of sin, which must be stopped in its tracks and not allowed to have its evil way.

But it is not the priest this time. There is a vigilante group which has taken on the holy role. So the lovely light-brown barks are tarred right up to head-height, a thick black tar falling and flowing in heavy gouts and globules upon the leafy ground. Thus love and nature are at once despoiled, and that crafty hoor, the devil, is forced to do his work elsewhere!

The platform dances are another story. These are joyous gatherings held at midweek and on Sundays over the summer months at some convenient crossroads a few miles out of town, and so within cycling or walking distance of the surrounding hinterland. Ours is at Farmers' Cross, where Cork Regional Airport now stands. It's a fine airy plateau looking down over the city and with miles and miles of rich green acres stretching away off to Kinsale in the south.

It is nothing at all to see hundreds of young people gathered there on the fine nights, for the most part the sons and daughters of local farmers or from the nearby villages of Ballygarvan, Togher and Pine's Cross. There is also a regular contingent out from the city, but the country folk tend to avoid them and keep their own company.

The platform is a concrete square big enough to take twenty or thirty dancing couples at a time and it's always full. The music is whatever happens to turn up: a button-accordion, a fiddle, a mouth-organ, occasionally an uileann pipe or bagpipe. They and the dancers make a bright and vibrant sound. Coming up the hill towards the Cross, you hear the music whirling and diving like swallows in the air with, in and out of it, the battering of boots and shoes on the platform, in time with the dancing beat. You'd have to be a frightful ould sourpuss indeed to think there could be any harm in it.

The dances are 'Céilí' and 'Old-Time', with the 'Military Two-Step' occasionally thrown in. There are good dancers and bad, peacocks showing fine feathers, young eagles spreading fine wings. As the music rides high and wild above them, it's a riot of dancing and swinging bodies – and all for the price of the few shillings it takes to pay the piper.

It so happens that I have a special interest in the Farmers' Cross platform: one of the local farmers, Fonsie Dan, has a big dairy herd and does a twice-a-day milk round in the city; his delivery-man is Declan and, for the huge reward of six-pence a week, I help him with the round. He is there, as are Fonsie Dan's sons and daughters, all hewn out of the red sandstone of south Cork or milk-fed from its honeysuckle fields – including the youngest, Joanie, with flowing red hair and the body of a glowing amazon. All the boys want to dance with her, but the one she wants is Johnny, one of her father's cowherds.

He doesn't wait to be asked. He is over like a shot when the next dance is announced and you can see by the way her hands go out to him that she's not at all unwilling. Away they go, partners in an eight-hand reel. When it comes to the swing, her skirt flies up, showing her wild and turbulent thighs. With one hand she tries to hold it down and Johnny pretends to look away, but the pretence doesn't work. You can see how thrilled he is by the great open smile that lights up across his face.

Rough and uncouth he may seem betimes, and you'd wonder why any girl would look twice at him; but now, in his fine new suit and his brown brogue shoes, what a dress-er he is! Besides, with that crown of black curls above his forehead, Brylcreemed and shining now for the platform night, he looks the picture of a prize young bull pawing the show-ring ground. Maybe that's what our budding Joanie sees in him? But he cannot have her for she is a rich farmer's daughter and he is the farmer's cowherd – and never the twain shall meet. Anyway, her big brothers, Dan and Jim and Tom, are there to see that she comes to no harm. But she knows – and her curly-headed bullring mate knows – that they each have a 'Joanie' in their own sights and can be easily ducked when she decides it's time to go. She hasn't the cut and wits of a teenage Eve for nothing. If it comes to self-defence, she'll be well able to look after her-self. It isn't exactly self-defence she has in mind though; and part of that 'looking after herself' will surely include making it to one of those woodbine-scented nooks Canon Cunnane is so fond of.

But suddenly it all comes to an end. The word is out that the platform dances are a threat to holy purity and a grave 'occasion of sin', so they are banned. This is done by the simple process of preaching them off the altar – nobody in the community at that time would dare disobey an edict like that. How the Church came to see the cloven hoof and the devil's work amongst the revellers at Farmers' Cross may not be all that difficult to understand: they had their own highly effective private and inbuilt research going – in the form of regular confession where the dark secrets are openly told. True, confessional secrecy is sacred, but there is no law against such information being anonymously pooled to come to this conclusion. So, to be fair to Canon Cunnane and his fellow-vigilants, they are not relying on hearsay; they have their own first-hand personal testimony – about where, when and how the deed was done and what led up to it. So, by the simplest of means, Joanie, Johnny and their like become the authors of their own destruction; and a lovely joyous feature goes out of our lives, never again to be restored.

But still, the love-game went on. Rosie Willie lived down the road from us, a petal-pink and lissom beauty who lit a lot of fires when she went by. To be smiled at by her set a pool of molten fire alight in the pit of one's stomach; to touch, hold or kiss her could happen only in dreams – and alas sometimes did!

A great deal was known, or said to be known, about how free she was with her favours, most or all of it in the imagination. Little was said, and that little with such brazen effrontery that even the bravest of the brave knew it was too good to be true. Out in the Black Ash beyond Turner's Cross one night, we're told, hadn't she 'led him on'; she 'had it in her hand' for him; then he 'got his hand up'; and, finally, as we slavered for the volcanic eruption (ah, genius for the fresh-minted word!) – 'She's a fabulous ride!'

We don't believe a word of it but as talk it's a surefire winner. So there is much sex in theory but little in practice, the risks being too great and the price too high when things go wrong.

Meanwhile, between those intrepid warriors who sang *Sweet Mystery of Life* and the crooning-and-swooning idols on celluloid, there is a whole unspoken, uncharted world of erotic fantasy, with desire and action fused in the imagination and in dreams – an uncouth and lusty beast marauding through the pastures of our virgin chastity. Like that song, the whole sexual caper seems to be full of the most elusive and seditious stuff, often suggesting that we know it all, yet not adding a jot to what little we do know:

Ah, sweet mystery of life, at last I've found you,
Now at last I know the secret of it all;

All the pining, waiting, wishing, hoping, yearning,
The tears of love, the tears of joy that fall.
For 'tis love and love alone the world is seeking,
'Tis love and love alone will find the way

Song-lyrics like that were so loaded with plaster-saintly perfection that, if you were to take them at all seriously, they would put you off sex for good. The most such angelic devotion could rise to was holding hands or a kiss, and that so chaste and pure that it might just as well be wrapped in flower-petals and embalmed until the disembodied lovers became angels and could then attempt to do the thing for real without the dreaded consequences

When Nelson Eddy finally got round to kissing Jeanette MacDonald in 'Maytime', we were all fast asleep and the month of May was damn nearly over. And when Clark Gable's 'Blackie' dressed her up as a show-girl in 'San Francisco', the good and holy Father Spencer Tracy took him to task for exposing her lovely parts – only to be clobbered for his pains by the unrepentant 'Blackie', a poor hoor of a nightclub owner whose only sin was that he was trying to turn an honest bob by the unlikely lure of La MacDonald in a mini-skirt.

The less real sex there was, the more eloquent and rhap-sodic were the songs about it:

Love, let me feel the thrill of your lips,
Love, let me feel the thrill of your finger-tips
As they linger lightly on my brow
And, darling, let me say – I love you.

So we are left swinging between impossible extremes, all starlight and roses one minute, all lustful and grotesque the next, until we don't know where we are, in hell or in heaven,

63

or maybe some love-bemisted purgatory in between, from which neither God nor man can rescue us.

While all this turmoil of sexual excitement and its rich imaginings are going on, our parents are at home, blithely oblivious to it. Or so it seems. In this, as in most other matters, our father takes the more sanguine and liberal view, being both by nature and experience a romantic himself and thoroughly disapproving of the negative approach – and certainly of everything Canon Cunnane and his kind stand for. As to the good man's prodding the love-sick hedgerows, Father would go as near as anyone dared to get out there and confront him; without doubt, he would be of the view that it must be a very curious and idle old man indeed who had nothing better to do with his time. Despite all the ravages and inroads into his own populous life, he can still get quite rhapsodic about the seeds and secrets of young love, and he has not forgotten that May day when, in the red tunic and black glengarry cap of the Dublin Fusiliers, he came down the steps of the North Cathedral under an archway of swords to possess his blushing bride.

There is not much of that mist-eyed fantasy left now. But occasionally he will come out with something which tells us it is still there. He will call her by her name – 'Julia'; sometimes, to our wild and stunned surprise, he will ask her to kiss him. Now we all love our mother, but kissing her in the way he has in mind, and the way she has come to be by then, would be about the very last thing any of us could imagine. It puts us all into a black knot of embarrassment in which we shut our eyes and try get out of there fast. But *in vino veritas* notwithstanding, we can see he means it. And, though we never hear him speak of that side of his life in the heartfelt cherished way he talks about the war and his old comrades, there is still clearly a stem of the old flame left, surely a feat of surpassing faith and loyalty from someone who has every reason to have put it well behind him.

For us younger children stumbling about in a world of innocence and confusion, in which sex and all to do with it is the forbidden fruit, those occasional love-moods of our father are in bleak contrast to the other times: when they live in mutual toleration, worse still in smouldering conflict; worst of all, when they turn on each other and fight with the same fire and passion that must once have gone into the making of us. The savagery of their mutual rage then descends upon our troubled house, tearing us apart in body and in soul. It is not a tearing apart that can be healed with words; only with time, which tells us that love and loathing sit side by side together all the time in many lives and only by the grace of God can they be got to remain bedfellows at all. That is why that half-ashamed, half-touched, fleeting kiss between our mother and our father is a sign of contradiction: that the love that fused in their uncanny union was but love in part; that the flame that kindled on a good May day on the Cathedral steps was blown out in the blast of the many bad nights that followed; but that its dim flicker would be fanned to life again and again to let them love – and live to fight another day.

Sometimes, there's a party in the house and there's drink and they all get to singing. One such night, big brother Ken sings that sickly-cloying lyric quoted above – 'Ah, sweet mystery of life, at last I've found you' – and Father nods and sighs and tries to mouth the words in mute encouragement. Mother looks daggers at him, knowing full well the 'mystery' he is thinking about – and hoping, praying, her innocent son isn't thinking the same.

For the sweet mystery of life that at last had found him

could mean that some designing rip has got her claws into her lovely boy and is leading him on in evil ways. Those ways would be away from God, the church – but first, foremost and above all else, away from her, an odd reversal of roles in which she assumes all primacy, forgetting that it was just such love that gave her the primacy in the first place. Having put in such a trojan fight for our survival over the long years, Mother lost sight of, or never conceded, that we might cherish other hopes, aims or desires. Love was a one-way track, its terminus always finally with her. The ultimate treason was another woman, an Eden Eve with a golden apple in her hand. 'Ye'll get enough of the sex yet' was but one part of this dark antipathy; it was an article of her faith – the mother of twelve conceptions, twelve parturitions, twelve branch-lines always leading back to her. The six who lived were her clutch of nestlings feathering up, she would make us strong and bright and beautiful – but for her eyes and her enchantment; that was a satisfaction huge and visible and certainly deep and wide enough to cover the travail and contumely of the years.

So, while our father sings the songs of love, loyalty and romance, our mother has other words for those songs, brushing aside his ardours with the ashes of poverty, disillusionment and the rags and tatters of a threadbare life. Those of us who lived – there's surely another story in those who died – are all children of that passion-filled and febrile house: consumed with love, torn apart by it, made by it and then unmade; but, with it and its siamese twin, sex, unable ever to look upon the world or live in it without its sundering, yet always healing, grace.

So it was with us and all or most of the people around us: trusting in the love of others to save our lives, encoiled with them and breaking free of them, and finally making it to some safe haven where, with luck, we could do what our fathers and mothers before us did: loved and lost, and sometimes loved and won, but always, with the losings or the winnings, making ourselves a life that would be nothing unless love had played a part.

But that's all away in the dim and distant future. First, we must 'the primrose path of dalliance' tread. Early glimpses of that path come with sylphs in school uniforms, pupils for the most part of the nearby holy and wholesome Presentation Convent on Douglas Street: Mary Bee, who dips her eyes when she's passing and then looks up with a wonderland of danger and invitation; ash-blonde Sylvia, tall and leggy, who trails her challenge past a crowd of us, knowing there is safety in numbers; Pat Clarke, fresh from the Sodom and Gomorrah of London town where some demon of iniquity has taught her how to tilt a beret on one side of her head so as to send out waves which tell us that, though but yet in her teens, she knows all about the sliver-shots of love and how to make and aim them.

My own first assault upon the seven-storeyed mountain comes with Rita, apple-blossom and the tint of roses, fourteen to my fifteen – at that age you get 20/20 vision to see perfection. She lives in Thomond Square down the hill from us and, like all the other girls, goes to the Convent School – which means that she must pass the bus-stop where I am standing every morning. From the moment she appears until she turns the corner into Douglas Street, this strange freezing thing gets me by the guts and won't let go. Is this what they call the pangs of love? Other fellows seem to be able to brazen it out, go up there and say – 'I fancy you and will you go out with me?' But I cannot do that. I would die first.

So instead I write her letters and poems – and never send

them. The poems are written by other people, with the words changed here and there and her name put in to make them sound like mine. They're sad, weepy poems dug out of books in the library and probably written by ould codgers in the last stages of senile dementia. They are the only thing that suits my mood:

> But if the while I think on thee, dear friend,
> All losses are restored and sorrows end.

One night at a Boy Scouts and Girl Guides rally, she sweeps past me in the line, looks over to where I am standing and smiles. God, what can it mean? That she likes me? That she could or would like me? That she'd like me better if she got to know me? Would, could, would – by the time I make it to bed that night, I'm praying to that God I invoked to please take a hand and do my love-talking for me. Ah, sweet mystery of life, at last I've found you! But God is at a safe remove and won't be press-ganged into anything so unholy. Though there is not, nor ever could be, the slightest hint of sex, that ugly and obstreperous beast.

Oh, there isn't, isn't there? One day, cycling towards me along Anglesea Street with the traffic all about her and she not seeing me at all, Rita's dress blows up in the summer breeze, showing the length of her honeysuckle thighs. I nearly die of love on the spot! I don't know what it is but, whatever it is, it has me hooked for life. I am fifteen, just about starting to shave – congeal it and bottle it and it will certainly last a lifetime.

Somehow, some way I have got to tell her; I cannot do it myself but I have this friend, a handsome blond little guy my own age and about to sprout a whisker too, who agrees to do it for me (like Antonio seeking the hand of Portia for his friend Bassanio in *The Merchant of Venice*, as I will shortly learn). He comes back to say what I already know: that she is beautiful and a stunner and all sorts of other wonderful things. I tell him I know, I know, but what did she say when he told her about me? 'She laughed and laughed,' he said. 'I thought she'd never stop laughing.'

Laughing and laughing is not what I want to hear, but it is all I am going to hear. Because in due course she has a friend who comes talking to me. And what this friend of hers tells me is that she does indeed fancy someone, but it is not me. It is the good-looking blond bastard I sent to plead my cause for me in the first place. Jesus, the bitter bite of it! There is a taste of dust and ashes in my mouth which will last forever.

But it has to be put up with, lived with, died with. Dying is a class option when you're fifteen.

As is evident, I do not die, I live. Somehow, the honeysuckle Rita goes down the tube of memory, never to return. Can it happen again? Will it? Unthinkable as it was then, it can and will; and, incredibly, the next time it will last. Now, most of 50 years on and with a flotilla of eight tied to its flagship, it is still afloat and looks like staying so now for what time is left. An enviable state, you say, in a world and a time much riven with strife and separation. Now at the biblical limit of three-score-and-ten, it is surely not my world anymore. Yet I may perhaps be permitted to express a view on it. It is this: with all the props and crutches, the ejector-seats and safety-hatches now available in this far more canny time, I ask myself how that flagship and its flotilla would have fared, had it been starting out on its maiden voyage now rather than when it did. It is of course a pointless question: we live in our own time, we get one go on the merry-go-round – and make the best or worst of it while we can.

In the meantime, I am glad that the bad things are

finished for good. It seems centuries now since that prying and puritan ould cod, Canon Cunnane, prodded the hedgerows with his blackthorn; the bullring Johnny can have his golden Joanie now for all he's worth after whatever passes for a platform dance; at least there's no need to worry about the consequences any more. Sex in a damp climate is no different from what it is anywhere else in the world; the holy preachers can preach all they like, there's no mad rush into the front pews to hear them.

One thing is sure: the love game will go on. Yes, I am glad the bad things are gone. Who isn't? All I hope is that worse won't come. But that's not for me in my time. The next in line can write their songs of experience when their turn comes. All I hope is that they don't come too easy or too soon, and that they leave a little room for the songs of innocence. They in their time were the honey-drop upon the fuchsia-bell, the piping of the April blackbird, the dews of morning upon the opening rose. They filled us with anguish and the folly of youth. Which, all foolishness be blessed, may now with luck become the folly of age.

5

Break the News to Mother

'The Lost Leader', 'The Uncrowned King of Ireland', 'The Chief' – Charles Stewart Parnell, leader of the Irish Parliamentary Party in the House of Commons at Westminster – died in October 1891. Our mother was then nine years old. It was a traumatic time in the life of Ireland. The Parnell Split went deep into political and community life, tearing whole families apart. The atmosphere is brilliantly caught in the family row at Christmas dinner in James Joyce's *A Portrait of the Artist as a Young Man*. For myself, I did not need to read that to know that it was part and parcel of the life and mind of Ireland at that time. To her dying day, my grandmother always wore the Ivy Leaf, symbol of Parnell, on her shawl on his anniversary day; and I remember her holding me by the hand as she pranced along the footpath on the Grand Parade to the marching band of 'Parnell's Guards', singing raucously the Parnell anthem in time with them:

> Let friends all turn against me, let the foe say what they will,
> My heart is in my country and I love old Ireland still.

Our own mother imbibed this with her mother's milk and never once lost sight of it. As a girl, she had once seen 'The Chief' in Blackpool – tall, bearded, cold, remote; in ways he would become for her the prototype of all patriarchal authority, her own stern father included. Her people stuck with him after the scandal of the divorce case – when, as one of the characters in Joyce has it, 'the priests and the priests' pawns broke Parnell's heart and hounded him to his grave'. It was that same old 'Nanny Apples' who once grabbed me by the arm and with ferocious intensity said: 'Never forget, child, that your people before you fought for Parnell with bottles in Blackpool!'

All that early life of our mother's was a turmoil of contentions and divisions, of foreign wars and home-grown outrages, of troubles in India, the Sudan, South Africa, as well as Fenian troubles at home, all of which happened on her doorstep because in one way or another, her own people continued to be involved. One uncle, Jimmet Fenton, was with the British general Lord Roberts in the famous routemarch for the relief of Kandahar in Afghanistan; another, Stephen Fenton, was part of an abortive invasion of Canada, then a British possession, by a force of Irish emigrants demobbed from the Union and Confederate sides in the American Civil War – and was charged with high treason against Her Sovereign Majesty, Queen Victoria, then also the monarch of Ireland. For that generation, having nothing much in the way of schooling to distract them, politics would become a main source of conversation and contention in their lives – and occasional hilarity as well.

For the half-starved, wholly enslaved people of Cork, it would be exclusively the politics of provision, of bread and circuses if they could get them; and, if not, the politics of war, not peace, because war, even if it brought death and destruction, brought soldiers' pay and separation money too. So well might a 'swaddy' of the Connaught Rangers sing from the trenches of no-man's-land:

> Don't be lonely, darling, I'll be coming back again,
> Before the pigs begin to learn to fly;
> With our separation money we'll be both as right as rain,
> When the old Sixteenth comes back to Athenry.

At the core and centre of all this, Mother was a young girl growing up, oblivious to it, yet part of it, but never having any other ambition than to live and grow, marry and have children, and then see them live and grow – the cyclic compulsion of ordinary lives, never noted for anything but that they had done just that: lived, died, and found enough vestiges of reward to make the in-between worthwhile.

We knew little or nothing about her early life and what little we did know did not come from her. 'God blast me schoolmis-tress', she'd say as she struggled myopically to draw a pen through the spider-tracings of her Christian name, Julia, the only word she would ever write. She was from that warren of lanes around the junction of Shandon Street and Blarney Street, a bleak and fetid world, riven with disease, malnutrition and death, where the best that could be hoped for was that the escape-route of the widespread infant mortality would give the blessed cherubs who died a brief glimpse of an unhappy world before their stem of life was snuffed out. Above their doomed doorposts a destroying angel might well have written: 'Abandon hope, all ye who enter here.'

Mother herself seemed to have had no childhood at all. All we ever heard was of a self-righteous and vengeful father, a mother who was enslaved to him, and brothers who fled home the first chance they got and came back years later, lost and broken men.

Her first happy memories seemed to have come when she was a little girl of eight, going out at dawn to work beside her mother in the flax-mill in Blackpool ('The Sunbeam' of later years). For her, it was the end of schooling and the start of adulthood. Educational enlightenment at that time stretched to the liberal extreme of 'three days on, three days off', the three off being used to feed a cheap labour market spent on the factory floor, sweeping the fallen flax and gathering it onto the carding tables. Half-past six in the morning until half-past six at night was the working day; the Ireland of that time was a full century behind those 'dark Satanic mills' of William Blake.

Contradictorily, Mother loved it and always spoke warmly of those childhood working days: going off in the dark mornings with her hand warm under her mother's shawl; the frost crystals cracking under their feet as they made their way along the pavements; meeting up with the other girls and women as the growing procession moved out towards Blackpool; the fright and frenzy when a crazy old coon, Denis Burns by name, mad from insomnia and the shell-shock of old wars, came clattering after them in hob-nailed boots as they fled to the safety of the flax-mill gate.

The factory horn sounded sharp at half-past six and the gate was slammed, leaving the stragglers outside until ten; apart from the terror of having to face the madman, they then had the added punishment of 'missing a quarter' of their day's pay. This indeed was the life of Blake's chimney-sweeps and the barefoot urchins of Wapping and the London dockside of Dickens. But for Mother it was a happy time, a time when she had a place in the world, with her friends and relations around her – a savage but salutary lesson in how little it takes to make a life. And, once there are no glittering prizes to distract you, how that little can be the heart and soul of it.

My best guess is that she stayed on in the mill until she married, and for several years after, when her bandbox soldier was away at one of his wars; surely a dull and boring time when the most that could be hoped for was the postman's knock and a letter with an exotic stamp from a foreign land. Where, when and how did she catch the dream that filled her later days? One glimpse of that black-and-white studio photograph taken a dozen years after that little girl had started to earn her keep shows the figure of a dignified and beautiful young woman, built for grace and good living, but with a star-struck look in her eyes that tells of a light and goodness she cannot have taken from the world around her. Was it there before she met her star-struck man? Some thrust towards the good, the excellent, before ever he arrived on the scene – even in those milk-teeth years when, as little more that a slave-girl, she swept the scraps and clippings from the carding room floor? Could it be that it was there, even in that very hell-hole, it was learned? A childhood idyll in an evil place, where, despite the grime, the sleeplessness, the calloused baby-hands, there was still the promise of a new and better time, the upward thrust which is the point and purpose of all our lives – the Dylan Thomas 'force that through the green fuse drives the flower'?

Other times would come when it would not be so: when the frost cracking under their feet would be the crackle of machinegun fire from the trenches of the Somme; when the

factory-horn and clanging gate would be the clang and boom
of the cannon in no-man's-land; when the songs they sang as
they went about their work would not be the fatuous jingo of
Colonel Blimp and his Empire-builders who told them to
'pack up their troubles in their old kit bag and smile, smile,
smile' – but the grim and savage lilting of the factory-girls in
Cecil Day Lewis:

> I've heard them lilting at loom and belting
> Lasses lilting before dawn of day;
> But now they are silent, not gamesome and gallant –
> The flowers of the town are rotting away.
>
> There was laughter and loving in the lanes at evening;
> Handsome were the boys then and the girls were gay;
> But lost in Flanders by medalled commanders
> The lads of the village are vanished away

Mother went on working in the flax-mill after she was
married; it was the one time in her life when she was briefly
a woman of substance. Besides her job, she had her 'separation money', the consolation prize of every soldier's grass-
widow. A woman of substance indeed, with a hundred gold-
en guineas in a savings-book. What was ten years of marriage without a man to that? By the time he finally came
back, the copper-coloured fusilier she did not know in the
march-past up the Grand Parade, she might indeed ask was
that the boy she had married ten years before; and for him,
was she the girl? That was 1909. There would be no more
partings, no more wars to keep them apart now anymore. Or
so they thought.

The following year, the first of the children, our big sister
Eily, was born. For a time she was an only child but that didn't
last. There is a blank between her and the other five who

survived; infant mortality and emigration were the tragic safety valves in those years. Mother never spoke about her dead children, except to say, when things were bad, that she had 'six little angels above in heaven looking after me'. If she had – and she truly believed she had – then they must often have had their work cut out seeing to it that the rest of us didn't end up with them. That we did not was due chiefly to her own tenacious grip on a life that, whatever else it might have, was surely not the heaven of her 'little angels'!

All that would come to pass in the no-man's-land of our mother's life between the time she was that girl of eight sweeping the flax-mill floor and the woman close on 50 I would come to know.

For this is where I come in – that waif creeping about on our tenement floor, and later the blue-eyed, fair-haired kid looking out upon our brave new world.

By now Mother is not the fine lady in the photograph with the coronet of black braided hair and the stylish cravat. She is a small sturdy dynamo with her hair tied in a bun and her sleeves rolled up, the powerhouse of all our lives. Of all the people around me, she is the one I am closest to but, young as I am, even then I know that her moods and fancies can swing like the cock on the weather vane, making it a tricky task to find a steady direction. She can be ferocious in defence of her own, even more so in attacking them: once, this shoe-last comes flying across the kitchen-floor – aimed at her own mother who was living with us at the time, making sure to miss her of course – love beating rage when it comes to aiming missiles like that. 'I'm very black,' she'll say when someone has hurt or belittled her; and 'Never the longest day I live will a single word pass between us.' If this happens to be someone near, a neighbour, a cousin, or one of her own, she'll top it with a gesture of surpassing despise: touching the tip of her finger to the tip of her tongue and sweeping the ghost of a spittle away, she'll say: 'Not as much as that will they get from me from this day on' – missing the point that 'not as much as that' has she ever to give! You don't want to cross her when she's in a mood like that; a wrong has been done – or imagined to be done, it's all the same – and she will not rest until it is undone. Mostly it has to do with the all-abiding evil, money, with our father as a prime suspect.

The slightest thing will bring it on. Sometimes, he'll come home on a Saturday night, all *grámhar* and loving and full to the gills with one of his maudlin war-songs. She knows this is Dinny Byrne's pub talking, which surely means he has won a few shillings on a horse. I can tell in advance that the cauldron is boiling by the way she keeps going to the door and looking out, hoping he'll be there and knowing he won't because if he was, the war-song would give fair warning. The dinner has gone cold and is stuck to the pot but it's left out as evidence of high treason; for good measure, when he does come, he says he doesn't want it, he's not hungry, to which she replies – 'Your belly is warm enough already.' With this, the clouds begin to gather.

Foolishly, he says it's not her money he was drinking, which she knows is true but truth has nothing to do with it; again foolishly, he blows the gaff on himself by saying it's money he has won on a horse, but this only adds fuel to the fire, since horse-money is still money; couldn't he think of her while he still had it? 'But you couldn't, could you, you coogled it and you kept it ['coogle' is from the Irish word *coigil*, to keep or save]. 'No wonder your belly is warm and your dinner is cold.'

Like all family rows, there is a self-generating propulsion to it: molehills become mountains and wrongs, past, present and future, come up. If they would only stop when they started, it would never start at all. I'm only a child and I know this; how can they not know it? Is there some devil in there driving them on? I don't want to be there but I stay because, foolishly, I think it is the only way I can stop them. But they start shouting at each other and then it's a shout too many and blows get struck. From the bleak and savage cavern of my helplessness, I cry out to them to stop, stop, for Jesus' sake stop, but the words get choked with the sobbing and there's blood coming up with tears from the middle of my heart. When he strikes her, it makes a sound like clods falling on a coffin and my crying is not from pain or fear but from the whole inside of me being torn apart. I hate him then and hate her more for the way she makes me hate him, but the bind she has on me has trapped me in her love ever before time began. The sound of my wailing brings them to their senses and they stop before they rend each other in pieces.

Of the two, she is the more shameless in exploiting my state, blaming it all on him. She says she'll turn all the children against him but, though I hate him, I do not want to be turned against him. In that sundering moment, I know all the horrors of domestic violence, the whole bleak and horrible case for separation and divorce. She leaves me no option but to side with her; I am her body more than his. If we could find some remote refuge away from there, that is where we would go. Of the two, he probably needs help and pity more – at least she has the family – but I feel no pity at all for him, only glad when he goes. I hear his slow steps going upstairs, dejected, beaten, an enemy retreating from the scene. Later, I hear him crying in the dark, a sad lonely sound like a whipped dog whining.

It will be years before I begin to have any real inkling

of his loneliness and grief; and years later than that again before I begin to feel that in seeking his half-mite of the nothing they have, he was asking no more than the least a loving man should have.

Yet it will pass and be forgotten, and better times will come. Against those embattled nights there are other times when they talk quietly to each other and even touch hands, as they sometimes do when they think no one is looking. Why can't it always be so? But it isn't, the bad side always seems to break through, until in the end there seems to be nothing but that.

And yet there is hilarity too. This mostly happens when people come home or are going away, great all-night parties – 'American wakes' they're called, except that by this time they're more likely to be London, Birmingham or Coventry wakes. There's always lots of booze about, for which God alone knows who pays and Mother is always in there in the middle of them; she can't be stopped singing once she starts.

There's always a party for her sister-in-law, Aggie Munn – oh, a very respectable lady over from Dagenham in a fur coat and stiletto heels. She runs a boarding house for Irish emigrants there; a hotel she calls it, others call it something else. In any case, it must make lots of money because the minute she comes through the door there's this great whiff of perfume in the air and, to add to it, great clouds of smoke from the cork-tipped cigarettes she smokes out of a long cigarette-holder; she'd remind you of those gangster molls in *Bonny and Clyde*. The only music she wants is blues, jazz and boogie-woogie and she jigs and jives her shoulder to the jig and jive of it. Mother says it would make you 'shit through your teeth', which can't be a very pleasant exercise, especially when it's your sister-in-law who makes you do it.

Mother has never forgiven her for the way she treated

her husband, Mother's eldest brother, our Uncle Johnny. He's the one who lost a leg with the Munsters in the Dardanelles and ended his days back home in Cork while Aggie went on to live happily ever after in London. Well, maybe it's wrong to blame her. What use was a one-legged Corkman running a grand hotel in London. Wouldn't he be far better off at home talking about the past with his friends in Cork?

But Johnny died and she got rich – and here she is now back every summer with her furs and her high heels, her jazz and her blues, and her long cigarette-holder, making Mother shit through her teeth. 'The longest day I live,' Mother swears, 'after how she treated my brother, not that much will I give her.' (Finger to tongue, spittle to finger, spittle away.) Aggie Munn doesn't look as if she needs 'that much'. She's a rich lady living it up in London, while Mother is still scraping the hapence together and wrapped up in a black shawl in Cork.

Still, Mother has the last laugh. Aggie dies – killed by the smoke from that chimney-stack sticking out of her mouth, Mother says – and it so happens there's this party going on in the house when the news comes. She calls 'Order' for herself, which makes people think she's going to make a speech or something, but it's not a speech, it's a song.

'Order now for meself,' she shouts; 'me sister-in-law is after dyin'' – which must be about the most unusual request for 'Order' that was ever heard. That's bad enough until we hear what the song is. It might not have been so bad if it was some sad and sorrowful thing, some dirge you would sing to bemoan the fact that your sister-in-law had died. But it's not, it's this:

Happy are we all together,
Happy are we, one and all,

That we may live a life of pleasure,
That we may rise and never fall.

Over in the far corner that night is another sister-in-law, Mamie Lane. Her husband, Mother's brother Thomas, was sent back from the trenches in the first year of the war, diagnosed with tuberculosis. That, you might think, showed commendable concern for the man's health on the part of his kind commanders, bearing in mind that, like millions of others, he was probably going to be dead in a short while anyway. But in those years TB could kill a whole regiment before ever the German Bren-guns got them, so he had to be shifted from there fast.

He came home to Cork, drew his pension for a bit and then died, leaving his widow, our Mamie, with the full pension of twenty-six and eightpence a week, a mighty sum and the envy of all the other war-wives and war-widows who, if they were lucky, got only half that.

Unlike Aggie Munn, Mother never has a hard word to say against Mamie Lane. She's pale and round like a ripe water melon and she has these great big eyes looking in front of her at some immemorial grief. The grief might have had something to do with her dead husband, but she never mentions him, only stares straight out with the ghost of a smile, especially if someone sings a song she likes.

The song she likes best is the one her eldest son, my cousin Johnny, sings. Mother loves this boy, but she says he's epileptic, which we all think is a grand thing to be, until we see him fall down and froth at the mouth and then have a spoon stuck between his teeth to prevent him from biting his tongue. We know then it's not a grand thing to be at all, but it's all over quickly and Johnny is back as if nothing had happened. He's a great favourite with everyone; Mother says he's the nicest boy in the world and she loves having him around. He calls her his Auntie Julie and he kisses her like a child, which none of us would dare to do, and when the party is at its height he stands between the pair of them, his mother and his 'Auntie Julie', he puts his hands around their shoulders and sings their favourite song which they both know is meant for them:

'Tis my mother's birthday today,
I'm on my way with a lovely bouquet
And she knows what that means to convey
For 'tis my mother's birthday today.

Then too there's the Sea Breeze Excursion to Youghal Strand. Aggie Munn is nothing to our mother when she dresses up for that. Father being in the railway, he can have free passes for the whole family and, since not much else comes free in our life, we always use them.

She puts on her navy coat and hat which some money-lender's largesse has enabled her to buy and she has this fox-fur thing around her neck with the cute little eyes looking out over her shoulder. A sight to see she is then, every bit as good or better than Aggie Munn, because she's younger and not all shrivelled up like a dried prune from the boogie-woo-gie and the cigarettes. Father is in his pressed suit, his bur-nished brogues and brown 'cuttaw' hat – a grand sight we are, with them in style out in front and the four of us younger ones behind. God bless the Sea Breeze Excursion and whoever invented it.

Youghal Strand is an hour away by train but a thousand miles in time. The first sight of the giant waves curling and crashing on the shore puts a knot in your guts, and the thought of getting in there to be swallowed up by them is an agony and an ecstasy. Father was a great swimmer in his day; there's a certificate in his Regimental Book for a three-mile swim he did in Malta. When we look out to the horizon we can see the round cap of Cable Island, miles and miles away.

'Could you swim out there?' big brother Jim asks.

'There and back and a lot farther and no trouble at all,' Father says. 'Will you come with me?'

Jim is a devil and will go anywhere with anyone once there's a thrill in it, but Mother puts on a sour puss and tells Father to stop the foolishness, the 'child' might get drowned. Getting drowned is a main concern of our mother's throughout the whole Sea Breeze Excursion day.

'How can he get drowned when he's only ankle-deep in water?' Father says.

But she keeps harking back to it until Jim feels there might be something in it after all, and before the day is out he might like to try.

After we arrive, Mother settles herself down against the breaker-wall and takes off her hat. But she keeps the coat and fox-fur on, which makes her stand out from the other women in the place. We're all thinking then – and our father is thinking it too: how we'd love to see her always like that! Aggie Munn can have all the hotels in London she likes, she'll never look as good or rich or handsome as our mother does now.

Her second major concern of the day, apart from us getting drowned, is making the tea. She has this primus thing which lights up like the gas when you pour the paraffin in. This boils the billy-can which is our kettle. After the tea is made, the billy-can becomes a pan on which the sausages are fried. They make a grand sizzling sound and our mouths are watering and, as quick as they're fried, down they go and more follow, fried or half-fried – it doesn't matter. There's sandwiches too and we know now what that word means because there's always sand mixed in with them. It's great eating with your bare hands and no table, with the waves crashing and the white surf running in, and the crowds of Cork screaming and shouting as they gobble down the sandwiches and sand-sausages.

Goodbye, Mother, goodbye all,
Goodbye, Mother, we're all goin' down to Yawl.

Then it's time for Mass. What Mass, we ask? We went to Mass this morning.

'It's your father,' Mother says. 'He wants to go to Mass.'

Our father doesn't go to Mass at home when it's just down the road from him, so why does he want to go now when he's in Youghal miles away?

'Ye don't have to come with us,' we're told. 'Ye can stay here and mind the clothes.'

This is good news. Now that we're fed, we're happy enough to stay around. But first Mother has a warning.

'Only let none of ye go near the water. Ye might get drowned.'

She calls Jim, who is a smart boyo and knows how to handle Mother and Father to his advantage when he wants to.

'You're to look after them till we get back,' she tells him. 'And mind now what I say: don't let them near the water; they might get drowned.'

Now he's the one who was going to swim to Cable Island with Father – if there's any one of us going to get drowned, it will be him. But he puts on his good face and Father slips him sixpence and says he's a grand boy and Jim smiles and says thanks and he'll look after us fine.

In any case, we're back in our clothes now and the towels are sopping wet, so there's no fear we'll risk getting drowned the third or fourth time.

So off they go arm in arm up the promenade, the fox's head looking out over Mother's shoulder at the pair of them – a cute little hoor of a fox who, although no baptised Christian like the rest of us, knows the 'Mass' they're off to. The minute their backs are turned, Jim does what we know from the first word he's going to do: gets into his togs and starts swimming for Cable Island. He's away out there bobbing along in the waves where no one can reach him, not even Father, who swam all those miles in Malta long ago – when there's this scream that would wake the dead because it certainly wakes him. It's our mother, back from 'Mass' already, with Father trailing along behind her. He seems to be in no hurry at all to jump in and save Jim from drowning on his way to Cable Island; Malta was a while back and Jim is at an age when, if the cold hasn't killed him already, he's not going to die of it in the few miles that are left. Stopped on his way to an Olympic medal by Mother's scream, he lumbers back in his fine strong trudgen stroke, and she gets him by the hair and shakes him and says he'll be the death of her yet if he doesn't kill himself first. But Father is smiling away quietly to himself and saying nothing and then, when her back is turned, he slips him another sixpence and says he's a good lad like his father before him – and will he please look after us a bit better this time.

So off they go to 'Mass' a second time up the promenade – only this time they have us bringing up the rear, my two older brothers Jim and John, my young sister Lil and me. What's up there at the head of the prom is 'Perks Amusements Park', with a merry-go-round, chairoplanes, swing-boats, a roulette table and a flying wheel with lots of geegaws to be won at it. Father tells Jim to keep us there till they get back from 'Mass' – and so he does, to the glad sound of the honky-tonk music mixed with the breaking waves.

For the sixpence we have a go on the horses and then he gets the four of us into a bumper-car and steers around, terrifying the wits out of the courting couples, who cling to each other while he's crashing into them for all he's worth to pull them apart. But soon the sixpence is gone and there's nothing left only time on his hands. This is a dangerous way to leave our brother Jim since, as we all well know, the devil makes work for idle hands.

There's this stand with small clay pots on it and if you can throw a wooden ring over one of the pots you get whatever is in it. One of them has a two-shilling piece, a mighty sum – we can see its silver face gleaming in the sun. It's near the edge of the stand with the canvas cover hanging over it, so no one can see what's coming at it from behind. Suddenly, Jim is gone, vanished as if the ground had swallowed him. Then we see a hand coming round the canvas cover and the pot with the two-shilling piece is gone. Then as quick as he vanished, he's back again and smiling at us, and away off we troop for another go in the bumper-cars and we're praying to God that 'Mass' will never end and we can be left in the care of our big brother, who will not be drowned on his way to Cable Island if there's any more entertaining way for him to kill himself.

At last the sun goes down and there's a wind from the sea and we're getting cold and tired and beginning to wonder when, if ever, this Mass is going to end. So we head back up the promenade hoping to meet them on their way back. But, as we're passing Clancy's, the pub on the strand, a boy comes out to us with bottles of lemonade; he says they're from a man and woman inside and we're to stand there and drink them and wait for our mother and father to come along in due course. The lemonade is a gift from God but it's gone before the boy is, so we follow him in to see who the

kind man and woman who sent it out to us are. And, lo and
behold, there they are in the Snug, the pair of them, him with
a pint and her with a medium, looking fine and pleased with
themselves.

And so we get on the train and head back down to earth
at the end of another fabulous Sea Breeze Excursion day.

That mother of Youghal Strand is a fine lady but she is a
stranger. She is not our Monday morning mother on her way
down to 'Davy Jones' Locker' with the coat, the fox-fur, the
pressed suit and the gleaming shoes, which will see us
through another week.

But this is the mother we know best – strong, determined, a fireball of a woman, caring for each of us as if we
were her only child, chastising us, shouting at us, sometimes belting the daylights out of us till we go in fear and
trembling of her, but always in her heart we know loving
us and leading us on to better things. And this is how she
will remain, ruddy with work, flinging out sparks of life
and light and hope, occasional sparks of fury too, but
always to make a new and better life for us all. She watch-
es over us like a tigress then and, whether in fear or favour,
in anger at being wronged by her or in terror of her ever
being taken away, she binds each one of us to her with the
knots and tentacles of a desperate, threatened love.

Sometimes things get the upper hand of her and she
says she's going to go down and throw herself in the river. I
lie in bed then stiff with fear that she will indeed do it. But
then the door bangs and I know she's back and I go to sleep
again. Or yet, drowsy with the scent of the Benediction
incense in the church, I am struck suddenly with the panic
of her being dead, shut up in a box and buried in a dark hole

where I cannot be with her. At times like that I know that life can never hurt or harm me except through her. And that neither pain nor loss nor any other injury at all can ever touch me as long as she is alive. She cannot, she must not, die – ever, ever, ever. How can she when she holds our whole world in her hand? And neither God nor man nor any living thing can ever put us apart.

Her single medium in Clancy's on Youghal Strand is wildly exceptional. In any case it's something we're not meant to see; that's why we're kept outside. It's against the law of God and man, God being the more important since drinking is more in the category of sin than bad habit – a distinction of some importance when you remember how hugely sin bulks in our penitential lives. How can she lecture us on the evils of drink if she is seen to be drinking herself? Besides, it puts her one up on Father when she gets at him about drinking the few shillings he has won on a horse. The trouble is that she has him trapped in this scheme of things as well as herself.   ›

Once, after big brother Ken had got that highly respectable job of his in the civil service, Father brought him down to Dinny Byrne's to show him off – and they arrived home hours later, singing the Dubs' war-songs and with their arms around each other.

'That's right,' she gets at him the minute he comes through the door, 'lead him astray with the cursed drink. You'll have the unfortunate child as bad as yourself by the time you're done!'

The 'unfortunate child' sensibly judges it best to remain aloof, leaving his defence to the more seasoned soldier. But Father pulls himself up with great dignity and swears that, as God is his judge, 'The boy had only a bottle of Bass!'

For Mother, smoking comes a close second in the order

of depravity. A boy who smokes is on the slippery slope; so brother Jim, who in all such matters will inevitably be the first offender, takes the precaution of locking himself – or so he thinks – into the small toilet on the stairs where he can blow the smoke out through the window by the simple means of standing tip-toe on the lavatory bowl. Virtue is its own reward and vice its nemesis: one day she's coming up the road when she sees the plumes of smoke trailing benignly skywards, whereupon she comes bursting through the 'locked' door and catches him red-handed. In the panic, the smoke goes down the miscreant's windpipe, half-choking him and bringing on a coughing fit which makes him slip from his perch into the bowl, where one of his legs sticks fast like a pheasant in a field, ripe for the cockshot.

Her attitude in this is only part economic: a packet of Woodbines costs twopence, the price of a pint of milk or a loaf of bread; but the moral factor is stronger. Smoking means young vice and an idleness of mind abhorrent to her sense of industry.

She can be quite violent about it. One Christmas Eve, we're coming home from town laden with the festive goods. These include a goose which I have grasped under my coat, its plucked and scrawny neck dangling through a hole in the pocket, and a bottle of raspberry cordial, treat of treats for us younger ones on Christmas Day.

But an even bigger treat will be the Woodbines. Brother Jim had managed to sneak off when Mother wasn't looking to buy a double packet of Woodbines for covert use by him and us throughout the holy season.

But in his haste he forgot about the matches. We couldn't risk taking hers: if she missed them, the secret would be out. The swinging goose-neck and the bottle of raspberry has my whole attention when I suddenly remember this fact.

'Jasus, we forgot the fuckin' matches!' I say – a strongish remark one may think coming from a ten-year-old – but, believe me, not at all unusual for us in that time. She swings round from where she is walking a few feet ahead. I can see the daggers in her eyes.

'What did you say?'

Brother Jim, quick as always to scent danger, is in like a shot to the rescue.

'He only said – "Jamus, we forgot the Friendly matches"'!' It is a brilliant piece of improvisation: his name is James, to us 'Jim', or 'Jimmy', very occasionally the Irish form 'Séamus': never, never in any circumstances at all, the extraordinary thing he calls himself now. And Friendly is indeed the brand name of the household matches we all use. But in his haste to improvise, he has forgotten one thing; for if we have forgotten 'the fuckin' matches', then what in the first place were 'the fuckin' matches' for?

She drags us into a nearby store whose owner she knows and can trust to keep silent in the ensuing flagellation. From experience I know what is coming and make a dash for it. But in the rush to get out, the hanging gooseneck gets between my legs and, striking at it to free myself, I let go the bottle of raspberry which crashes in smithereens on the stone floor. So we now have financial on top of moral ruin. Her rage is at its height now but, with all the Christmas stuff, her hands are full, so instead she kicks out at me. But fortune favours the bold; her foot slips on the raspberry-wet floor and down she comes in a pool of moral turpitude which will surely guarantee us a very merry Christmas indeed!

At last our father dies and she has us all to herself. We are no longer children by then but we are still helpless against her possessive forays. Girlfriends are resented as if they were predators, scheming to get at us and get us away from her; marriage, when it comes, is the ultimate treason, a reneging on the lifelong bond she has with us. This attitude of exclusive possession will be communicated in sulks and silences, in sudden fierce hints of deception and flashes of wounded indignation.

A man can, we are told, have several wives but only one mother; one wonders what suddenly became of the lifelong marriage-vows – but then they carry small weight when put in the scales beside a mother's love! For a woman not much given to poetry – or any other kind of reading either, apart from the Deaths column in the *Evening Echo* – she suddenly comes out with the most alarming and macabre verses, some with echoes from Father's long-forgotten wars:

Break the news to Mother,
Tell her there's no-one other,
There's no-one else but Mother,
No matter where you go.

We squirm at such shameless press-ganging on our affections, but that doesn't put her off. Death is a great winner, its dark muse quick to her lips whenever any of us attempts a getaway:

A mother's love is a blessing, no matter where you go,
Keep her while she's living, you'll miss her when she's gone;
Love her as in childhood though she be old and grey,
For you'll never miss your mother's love till she's buried
        beneath the clay.

Still, she is getting old and the frequency with which she comes out with such darksome verses has hints that mortality is on her mind. She sleeps less, a habit not unconnected with the fact that Jim, now a bus-conductor, has to be out at all hours to take the early morning service to the country fairs. All the wild habits of his boyhood have coalesced now into the wild habits of manhood, so he'll come home at midnight, poleaxed from drink and exhaustion, leaving strict orders to us to get him up in time; orders which we all promptly forget – all but her. Then out of the depths of our slumbers the bus will come throbbing and shuddering up the road. Everyone in the street, not to mind the house, will be shaken to life – all except him; having safely delegated the task of waking him, he sleeps soundly on. Then all of a sudden the house becomes a wild circus, with 'Jesus, Jesus in heaven' being imprecated to get him up. 'He's here, he's here, get him up for Jesus' sake; he'll be sacked!'

This is a disaster of such cataclysmic proportions that, no joke, it will be the black ruin and destruction of us all. Through the fog of sleep and shattered dreams, dark stories about life on the dole and death in 'pagan England' suddenly and alarmingly come to mind. The house is wide awake now, with lights and shouts and windows being flung up and down, while the leviathan throbs and shudders at the door. But the sleeper sleeps on, blithely unaware.

At last he comes to and by some hand unknown to himself or us gets into his clothes and is finally bundled out into the raw morning air, with Mother bringing up the rear with bread and rashers and cups of tea. But she's too late: the leviathan is already rattling and chain-sawing its way up the road, with him hanging on and the driver, Billy Lynch, calling the curse of God down on all the snoring, drunken mates he has ever had the misfortune to work with.

Then suddenly all is silence. Like the 'knocking at the gate' in *Macbeth*, Duncan is murdered, the deed is done, we can all go back to sleep.

We all do – all but her. The habit of dawn-rising, which the little girl of eight had from the flax-mill days, has never quite left her; but with the hammer-blows of years, it has taken its toll, mostly in a kind of moping vacancy in which increasingly she sees what is going on but only vaguely takes it in. I, being the last of the brood, am at home a lot with her and can see the vapours gathering. When I come in from school in the evenings, there she is at the window, looking out for the familiar faces and footfalls that have measured all her days. Most of them will not be coming this way again: not her whipcord mother, wrapped up in a shawl, her flinty face cutting the east wind; not her bandbox fusilier, who has left her now for service in a continent farther away than all the Africas he ever knew; not her 'six little angels', who never knew the bad times the rest of us would know because they had the luck, or ill-luck, to get out in time. Gone now are the days of the zinc tub full of clothes in front of the kitchen fire and her strong arms kneading them; gone the summer days when the winter blankets were stripped down and plunged in to be washed and turned and wrung and hung out on the line to dry.

These are the twilight years when she is sitting at the window, shuffling about in a half-trance, eyes glued to the Deaths column, praying fitfully, moving the table-things from place to place just for something to do – all that ineffectual mobility which is an early sign of decay, a body exhausted, a will that is not. To the mute accompaniment of her thoughts and sayings, daily regurgitated and recycled, I become bored to distraction by their repetition and fall asleep over the table as she talks. When I come to, there she is back at the window, watching the world go by, knowing, as all people whose active life is over must know, that this time of peace so often longed for is a bad second to the time when all the waking hours of day and night were filled.

Sometimes, later on in the night, we sit around the fire and, more from idleness than affection, the younger of our sisters, Lily, begins to comb her hair. The long tresses hang about her shoulders – just as they might have done for that beauty in the photograph long ago – silken, shining and still quite remarkably black. 'Amn't I the nice little girl now?' she purrs audibly at the unaccustomed care. Her moods are calmer; death and dying often come up, and emigration is another regular theme; both figure in her growing repertoire of songs. These seem to flood back as the tide goes out, Famine-paeans of godawful calamity, with half the neighbours weeping at a party by the time she's done:

> Oh, look at the big ship a-sailing,
> It is bound for some far-distant shore;
> And listen to the cries and the wailing
> For the land they will never see more.
> Some cry for their wives and their childring (!)
> And more for their sweethearts at home,
> For no more they'll return to old Ireland,
> The loved land, the Irishman's home.

I am by no means certain that these masochistic celebrations have not affected my own view of life which, though normally calm and well-adjusted, can occasionally lurch into sudden and alarming bouts of tearfulness!

But as to our mother, there is another not-so-sad-and-weepy mood; this is the assertive side, the mother-of-all-I-survey, which comes out whenever one of us tries to stop her stop her shouting about how she has brought us up against the odds.

'What have ye to be ashamed of?' we'll be asked. 'What have ye to hide? That yeer mother never went to school? Well she didn't. That she can't write her name? Bad luck to me schoolmistress, she can't. The lanes of Shandon Street and the flax-mill in Blackpool – that was my school. And now ye're all reared and high up in the world and yeer father is dead, why wouldn't I shout? Haven't I every good reason to shout and be proud at the end of me days?'

Some day, somehow, this is going to blow up in our face. As ill-luck will have it, it happens the day I get married. We can all see it coming, can see too there is no way of stopping it. There is wine at the meal, at that time and in our life an unaccustomed beverage; furthermore, it's white, the colour of water, hence to be drunk at will with no ill-effects whatever. Inevitably, sooner or later, from old family custom the singing will start; again as ill-luck will have it, one of the songs is Puccini's 'Oh, My Beloved Father'; there is a devilish miscontrivance in such things.

Suddenly, at the sound of the word 'father', she's up and away. From where I am in the room, I can hear her cut loose from the arresting hands.

'It's their father would be proud of them this day, a man with nothing but his four bones – not like all the grandees I have about me here. Who's goin' to stop me?'

I flee the scene and make for the bar, but can hear her still going full blast even down there. She bursts into song herself; it's one of Father's old war come-all-ye's:

All around the shanty table,
Sitting with a social few,

Nothing else could be more pleasant
Than those few hours I spent with you.

Happy are we all together,
Happy are we one and all,
That we may live a life of pleasure,
That we may rise and never fall.

It's October, the last days of the month; early winter frost is edging the leaves and by six in the evening it's already getting dark. In the holiday village up in the mountains where we're going to stay, there is this old churchyard full of tumbling and moss-covered headstones. Is it some preternatural love of death and disaster that brings me to such a place on my wedding day? But as I walk with my new wife amongst the old stones, trying to make out the names of the long-forgotten dead, it is not they who come alive inside me but the sound of her wild and raucous voice.

Oh yes, she is all she said: a child of the lanes and the flax-mill, garrulous, truculent, proud of her achievements, drunk now on the strength of it, and in all probability sleeping it off somewhere in the full view of everyone, having exhausted herself with her passion for grief and her even more grievous passion for gaiety. Yet it is none of those things that's in my mind on that late October night, but at long last the fear with which she has held me ever since the day I was born: the fear of her footfall fading in the world, dying like the leaves of summer now shrunk and shrivelled on the ground. I know then that nothing she ever does can turn me against her; and I know that when she goes, nothing will ever again fill the place she has for me in the world.

But go she does, as we all must, though not before having one last laugh at us all. Her four sons do indeed carry her coffin down 'Evergreen' to the parish church of Christ the

King in Turner's Cross. It has been her lifelong wish, frequently and ardently prayed for; she couldn't be dead soon enough to cash in that final cheque upon our love. I am one of four, the last – to begin with undoubtedly a mistake.

I thank her and her bandbox fusilier for it. For me, for them too I hope, it was a most rewarding folly.

6

NANNY APPLES

NANNY Buckley, our mother's mother, was two women and came twice into my young life. The first was a dark cavern with black pots and a kettle boiling on the hob, a place with a low ceiling, a dusty floor and white-washed walls with big holes in them full of treasure for probing hands: coins and beads and coloured combs and bone studs for men's shirts and, best of all, the knocked-off heads of statues, Blessed Virgins, Sacred Hearts, Infants of Prague and Little Flowers, crimson and blue, gold and glitter, and absolutely smashing for marking out hopscotch lines on the footpath outside the front door.

Our grandmother was lord and master of this cavern and, when she was there, we crept about like mice, fearful of making any noise that might draw her eye on us. It was on Bachelors' Quay beside the river Lee; why Bachelors' I can't make out because there were no bachelors there, only old men who had been gobbled up by their wives and women a long time ago.

When the wind got up and howled with fury under the

North Gate Bridge, the waves reared up like fanged wolves and flung themselves on each other in a wild commotion that would all but drag me in. I would cling close to the quayside bars then and step by single step make my way to the calm centre near the eye of the storm – behind the front door of Grandmother's cavern home.

Then we shifted to this new house on the far of the city and I never saw that grandmother again. But one day, a long time later it seemed, this small gnarled person comes to the door, Mother brings her in, gives her tea and cake and things and tells us to come up and hug her. She says, 'She's your Nanny'. But we know she's joking because she's not, she just can't be, without the black pots and the kettle boiling on the hob in the cavern where she was lord and master; she's not the Nanny we knew, this woman, with her hands hanging with nothing to do, her shawl loose about her shoulders and her grey head bare above it like a Red Indian's tomahawk.

After that she comes every day and I get used to her; I even get to like her. At least I don't go in fear and trembling of her as I did of the Nanny on Bachelors' Quay. And bit by bit I begin to tumble to it that she's there for the same reason we're all there: that Mother is strong and powerful and none of us can ever live anywhere but where she is.

And very good to her Mother is, too. You can tell she loves her by the way they make it up after they've had a row. But, boy oh boy, what rows! They are the bad times for us all, with fierce strange names and curses being flung about, like 'heartscald' and 'hoor's and bitch's bastard' and other things that must be bad because they spit fire at each other when they say them.

Grandmother stalks out of the house then with the shawl up over her head. She says she knows when she's not wanted and she'll never darken our door again – which I'm praying to God she won't because if she does it'll be the same black ruin of us all over again. But back she comes the following day as if nothing had happened, this time with the shawl down on her shoulders and her head free above it and Mother takes her by the hand and brings her in and there they go talking and laughing and making tea for each other like a pair of old pals, till you'd think that nothing will ever come between them for the rest of their lives.

I'm all of eight when that Grandmother comes to live with us; she is eighty. By all the laws, I shouldn't like her: she's wrinkled and bent and gummy, like a witch you'd run from because in a fit of rage she could grab you and gobble you up. But I don't run. I stay. In fact, being the youngest of the family, I'm with her a lot and get quite fond of her. 'Love' is a word we use only about God or the Blessed Virgin or some of the saints we're supposed to pray to, but that's the strange feeling I have when she has me by the hand under her shawl on the black mornings as we trudge off down town together – like that Ruth in the Bible we saw at the pictures in St Mary's Hall, all lost and forlorn in the desert with only her child's child for company.

What she was before coming to us was a fruit-dealer. Young as I was, I well remember her from those days, with the fruit-trays propped up on orange-boxes all around her under the fountain near the North Gate Bridge. It's a trade she never lost touch with.

Now, when her trading days are done, she never comes home to us empty-handed. She always has these little secret stores of apples and oranges, bananas and pears stashed away in the large canvas apron-pockets, which were the coin-boxes of the fruit-trade in her day. And with what cunning she can use them to effect! The tactics of bargain and barter she still has at her fingertips and since there's nothing now left to bargain for but the prize of our small delight, she bargains for that with a deadly guile. From the minute she arrives in the street, all the children of the place come swarming about her, clawing at the canvas pockets, knowing for sure there's something there, while she's letting on there's not. She makes a great show of shoving us away then; she huffs and she puffs and let's on she doesn't know what we're looking for, but that doesn't put us off, only makes us clamber and crush about her even more. And so it goes on all down the street, with shrieks and shouts and yelps following her all the way: 'Any apples? Any apples? Any apples?'

So, with time and the constant sound of it, she becomes 'Nanny Apples', the name she will be known by for the rest of her life.

She has nothing left in the world now – the cavern on Bachelors' Quay is demolished, her man and her children are gone, her days are spent between our house and our Uncle Jimmy's across the city; nothing left but those daily pockets of russet apples and yellow pippins and over-ripe scarred pears that no one with any real money would buy. But in the beehive world of our tiny lives, the fame of her riches spreads far and wide, and we children of that time and that place will remember her coming like the Coming of the Magi, an epiphany rich with golden opulence. And as we munch upon the juicy fruit with houndstooth relish, her eyes light up with approval and her gummy jaws munch in unison. A rose of the world she is for us then, our youth and her age blended in a single sunray of delight – and all for the price of a few useless unwanted things, bringing light and life into useless but not unwanted lives.

She came from a tough breed. Her sister, 'Aunt Ellie', is tall, stiff and elegant, a woman in black like that old servant in Bela Lugosi's 'Dracula'.

She is younger than Grandmother but has the same clenched and fearsome jaw. Her husband, one Mick McGrath, is long dead by this time, but not before producing a brood of tall, dark and handsome men and women who, whenever I see them later around the streets, make me wonder how blood relations can be so bloody unalike! One of them, Jackie, is a commissionaire in the Savoy cinema, a post of great importance judging by the gold braid on the peak of his cap and golden tassels dangling from the epaulettes on his broad shoulders. What's more, we know he's important – can't he walk right down the line when he sees us in the queue and pluck us out to bring us in, scot free! His brother, Mick, is also a man of importance. He's a petty officer in the British Navy. Well, anyone can be an ordinary old officer, but to be a petty officer, that must really be something.

Their sister, Annie, is tall, dark and handsome like her brothers but she does nothing for her woman's looks by topping herself with a pudding-bowl hat and carrying a stiff black umbrella – a sure sign, our mother says, that she's a 'Lay-de'.

Quite the most remarkable of the whole brood is Grandmother's brother, Jim. Known as Jimmet, he's a paragon of square-bashed elegance. Long ago he was with the British Army in India and to this day wears the stiff wing-collar and bowler hat of the men of those days – men who knew their place in the world. A pretty lofty place too in the slack civvy world of the Cork to which he came back. He has this job with Murphy's Brewery which makes him one of the elite of the working class, in proof of which he still dresses with the rigour of his Indian Army days.

Even as an old fellow, he's still quite the peacock as he struts along Patrick Street and the South Mall on Sunday

103

morning, the living picture of 'the sergeant-major on parade'. By all accounts, he has reason to be on parade. Once there was this famous forced march in Afghanistan for the relief of a city called Kandahar, a great military feat by common consent, for which its leader, Lord Roberts, a Waterford man, would earn the endearing title 'Bobs of Kandahar'. It was twenty odd miles a day for twenty days in blistering heat, some feat then or at any time and certainly something for a man who took part in it to crow about. But you mustn't crow too loud in the presence of other crowing cocks, especially ones who in their time saw their own Kandahars and maybe worse. Sooner or later, one of them is going to take up the challenge and crow back.

It happens on the day of Grandmother's funeral when, in the front row behind the hearse, Jimmet is walking – marching would be nearer the mark – with our father and some of his war-comrades, who of course are much younger men. It's a steep climb to the top of Blarney Street out to the Curraghkippane, and Jimmet, in his eighties, knows it. But the stiff collar and the bowler hat are still there, and Bobs of Kandahar is still stepping it out with the best of them when suddenly the pace gets too hot and his breath gets shorter and soon he's puffing and blowing fit to kill.

'Where's Bobs of Kandahar now?' one of them cruelly asks.

'He's here, by Christ, and still marching' comes the fighting answer. 'Which is more than ye young bastards will be when it comes to yeer time!'

In her early days Grandmother, the fruit dealer, did the country fairs and markets, with frequent forays to strange places with fantastic names – Dripsey, Duhallow, Kerry Pike, Carrigtoohill – places of magic and mystery which we dream about but will never know. There she is, trussed up in her black shawl, sitting astride the shaft of her donkey-and-cart, our Mother Courage out in the frosts of morning and back home at night when the city lights are on. But she is stronger and braver than any of us; and the wind tearing the branches and the hail slashing the rising corn are not the black enemies we think, but the voices of familiar friends to keep her company along the way.

Her husband, our grandfather, is dead by my time. All are agreed that in his time he was a rigid man. If, as people say, the Ireland of that time was a great big matriarchy, it left him and his likes with a very soft option: so long as the matriarch did the work and the earning, he could stay at home to deplore the evils of the modern world and applaud the virtuous who stood against them.

Home she would come after a long day on the roads, the canvas pockets heavy with the coppers of her trade, to find the door locked and barred against her: it wasn't proper for any woman to be out so late. If she was, she was up to no good.

Our own mother never forgot those early days: the 'fallen' woman outside the locked door, the sobbing followed by silence, as the white-slave wife, wrapped in her shawl, huddled in under the outside stairs in terror of her stern and righteous husband. Then one of the boys, Mother's brothers, could take it no longer and he'd rush to the door to let her in. At this, the Great Patriarch would unbuckle his leather belt to teach him a lesson in parental obedience. But it would be too late, or the boy would be too quick, for she'd be in and, as the belt began to fly, she'd be on him like a tigress, ferocious now in defence of her own as, a moment before, she was submissive to protect them.

Such is the mark that this left on our mother's life that when her time came, she would never let our father lay a finger on any of us.

Anyway, at last he died and Grandmother was on her own. Nothing remained of him but the memory – that and a framed picture of a solemn man with cold eyes and a face of stone looking down from the wall above her bed. Being our grandfather, we hoped and prayed he would find whatever heaven he was bound for; but at least on earth from then on, the little woman who kept him could travel the roads in peace, knowing that the door would be open and the fire lit when she got back.

All that Hogarthian tumult of life and death and hand-to-mouth provision was well over by the time I came along. It is easy to fantasise about it now; at this distance it's an all but forgotten memory. In any case, it never touched me at all; there were always willing hands to see that this particular morsel of humanity got fed. What can be said, though, is that the 'hard-work-never-killed-anyone' message which we were always hearing certainly did not kill her. And there were still few years left. Those were the years of the cavern on Bachelors' Quay, of the fire red in the grate and kettle boiling on the hob. But then this centre-city slum clearance plan comes along and Bachelors' Quay is no more.

Grandmother is moved out lock, stock and barrel, including all the headless Sacred Hearts, Blessed Virgins, Our Ladies of Perpetual Succour and Blessed Martins de Porres (a black man, but she forgave him that, being one of her own beloved Dominicans on Pope's Quay).

From then on she divided her life between us and our Uncle Jimmy's and became the 'Nanny Apples' we all knew. In some ways, it was a good time for her: she had her two pensions – the Irish one and one from her husband's time with the British Army; but it was a lonesome time too, with the children and the grandchildren mostly gone and her memory stuck like a stopped clock in the heyday of her life.

I was too young to understand all that, unaware too that it had happened before, as it would surely happen again. I would come across her sometimes looking out the window with this half-moaning, half-crooning sound. 'Give over that old ullagoaning', Mother would say. But she'd take no notice, just go on – a kind of praying and singing to someone who was there and yet was not.

It would be years before I saw the like again and heard the selfsame sound. That was at the Wailing Wall in Jerusalem where old men, oblivious to all but some deep, impenetrable grief within them, bowed, nodded and mumbled in the same hypnotic ritual. To me, an outsider, it looked comic; for them, as for Grandmother, it was coming from somewhere and something at the very core of their lives.

I was to see other women like my grandmother in other places: in the steaming fetid sidings along the roadways out of Bombay, where whole families, young and middle-aged and ancient, squatted in the dust and mud; in the alleys and doorways up from the port of Xiamen in South China where black-shawled crones the spit and image of her crouched from their wicker chairs over a red fire; in the backways of Hong Kong, stricken with half-starved Chinese; in the cobbled lanes shimmering with equatorial heat up from the docks in Mauritius; in the hovels and mud-huts among the paddy-fields all along the road from the seaport of Tianjin into Beijing. Nearer home too – in the packed and steaming lanes below the rich villas and towering tourist blocks in what were once the little fishing villages of Iberia and the Mediterranean – and nearer still in the lanes and hovels of the forgotten places in our own dear island home. And they were always the same: bent and knotted like a weathered blackthorn, hard as ebony, and with the fierce black eyes of the indomitable survivor.

I salute her in them and know that she and they would have understood each other well: the same struggle for a toehold upon life, the same animal instinct for the protection of their own, the same implacable courage dragged up from God knows what source of strength to see that they got a better deal.

And I like to think that they manage a smile of recognition, which tells me that they know what Grandmother knew: that the fight is worth it; that the pain, the anguish and the deprivation will pass, but the courage and the rewards will not; and that some day, some place, a child or children of theirs may come to know that such a time was lived so that they might have a better life in the world.

Anyway, for Grandmother, it all came to an end one day as she was making her way across the city to Uncle Jimmy's place on the North Side where she was staying the night. A whistling messenger-boy on a bicycle came by and, with no time to miss the small black shawled woman darting out in front of him across the road, he hit her, head on, and knocked her out cold. It was a fall that would have killed a woman half her age but it did not kill Nanny Apples. Instead, after a minute or two, she was up and away – and that might have been the end of it but for the following morning when our uncle hears this half-strangled sound coming from her room; he goes in and there she is on the floor, speechless and paralysed.

The Little Sisters of the Assumption are sent for and they

come and look after her from then on. For the first time in her life she has some inkling of what the word 'luxury' may mean. When we go to see her, she is propped up on the pillows in a fine white nightdress, her hair combed and plaited and her tomahawk head at rest, completely relaxed. A very picture she looks in all this finery – but it isn't her at all. It can't be, lying there speechless and still and depending on other people to keep her alive, when she had spent the whole of her life doing that for them.

From then on, we await word daily that she has gone but word does not come. What does come is the news that she's rallying and, sure enough, when we next go to see her there's this glint in her eye and a steady rumble deep down in her scrawny throttle which says that she's going to make a fight for it.

When I come in close to her, her good hand darts out from under the bedclothes to grab me, but I duck, remembering strange stories about wicked witches who grab little boys to carve them and eat them up. But then I remember that same hand holding mine under the warm shawl on the winter mornings and I think – will it ever be like that again!

So summer passes to autumn and autumn to winter, Christmas comes and goes and day by day she edges back. First her voice muttering things some say they can understand but I can't; then it's the good hand reaching out for the little things she needs in the small darkened room that has now become her world.

Then suddenly, with no warning, one cold January morning there's this urgent knocking at the door and, when Mother goes down to open it, she sees Uncle Jimmy and he's crying ... So back we go with him across the city and there she is right enough, laid out by the Little Sisters – a painted doll, I declare, with the blue and white habit of a 'Child of Mary', though no habit or anything else can change the look of that tomahawk head. You can be sure she put up an almighty fight against having to go.

We go on our knees beside the bed in the usual way and begin to pray. But I keep one eye on her hands twined in the Rosary, the other on that set and fearsome jaw. Dead she might indeed be – but with Grandmother you could never be sure.

So, with her brother Jimmet and the other men doing their 'Bobs of Kandahar' best, we troop out behind her up to the Curraghkippane above the Lee, where all her people before her are buried. It's a quiet place looking down over the river, the main road to Killarney a few hundred yards below. There is a great big roadway there now with double-artics flying up and down at all hours of the day and night; but there was a time when the only sound was the beat of a donkey's hooves in the dawn hours as our 'old woman of the roads' passed by to make a better life for us all.

We have come a long way since then, the children, the grandchildren, the great-grandchildren of our embattled Mother Courage. It would have been good if she could have known a little of all that while she was still around, that the candle burning in the shaft-lamp beside the donkey's rump was lighting the way for our bright new world. But she didn't – isn't that why 'promised lands' are such a cheat?

But whatever in any of us has spirit and life, whatever has love and loyalty to our own, some of it must surely have come from her. So does the spirit live on though the puny body dies. And so may a young boy's hand, warm under an old woman's shawl, stay warm now until his own time comes.

7

Oh, Death, Where is thy Sting?

NANNY Apples was the second mother in my life. As I said earlier, there was a third; I will shortly come to her. But the truth is that this was all a woman's world: women were about me everywhere. In that fourth-floor eyrie of Willie and Winnie's, as in the cavern that was Nanny Apple's home, it was the women who were lords and masters; all the important things were said and done by them. There were other women, other Mothers and Nannies in and out of our lives all the time, shawls down on their shoulders or arms akimbo above the washtub, a long progress of ancients finding comfort and solace in each other and, in whispers incomprehensible to the rest of us, telling each other about the dark doings in other people's lives.

Auntie Nonie, Father's only sister, was without question the fattest woman in the world. She lived in Drummy's Lawn at the foot of Shandon Street, a great sonorous round of woman, with cohorts of fleshly grandeur following in slow motion her every step. Such was the pace of her galleon passage that she would have to pause for breath every few

steps to gaze out upon the world with bloodshot aquamarine
eyes. She too was a fruit-dealer and kept her stall under a
tumbling and dusty wall opposite Lorton's clothes-shop.
Being right beside where we lived in Goulnaspurra, she
would never let me pass without stuffing some of her wares
into my pockets. When the day was done, she would gather
up what was left into two great panniers, to be tied with
straw ropes across her back and swagged up the hill to
'Hallo's' pub on Shandon Street. There she would fill the
snug with ample pride and put away quarts of brown ale
until closing time. 'That ale will be the death of her yet,'
Mother would say. Knowing her death-wish on drink, that's
what she'd say anyway. But in the end she turned out to be
right. Or nearly so. When we went over on the August
Sunday morning of her death, her daughter Mary, who lived
with her, weepingly pronounced her cause of death: 'Tripe
she ate, Julie girl, after she had her fill below in Hallo's last
night. And, Jesus help her, she's payin' for it this mornin'.'

Nanny Apples, Sumo Auntie Nonie, scarlet Aggie Munn
with her lipstick and stiletto heels, Mamie Lane stunned into
a trance by some immemorial grief – those and others were
in and out of our lives all the time: with shouts and shrieks
and cat-astrophes of birth, death and marriage, with inter-
minable cries and prayers and novenas for help from God or
saint or anyone else who showed the least sign of being able
to help them – with money mostly but other things too: a job,
a house, an errant son to be spirited away before the law got
him, a good son gone of his own accord to foreign parts from
which he would not come back. The praying was as pas-
sionate and intense as it was helpless: caught up in a world
where the options were few and the outlets nil, neither God
nor saint nor man could keep up with the daily run on their
litany of imprecated favours.

May Drummond and May Lucey formed another small cluster in our galaxy of stars. They lived in a red house hanging over the river with a flight of steps up to the front door. By now, it was a tottering doll's house of a place which in times past must have seen its days of grandeur. This was before the river banks were built and boats could pull in there, like the gondolas in Venice at full tide. Even still, when the river was in flood, this pair would be marooned above the waterline, like the occupants of Noah's Ark, waiting for the deluge to subside.

'Awrigh' so', May Lucey would keep on saying whenever we were there on a visit; they were the only words we ever heard her speak. A docile, compliant creature, always bowing and bending as if she wasn't quite sure she was meant to be in the world at all.

May Drummond had a face like a ripe apricot and was old enough to be her mother. Maybe she was? She was always giving us children sweets, sugared rock and candied apples, and once, when we remarked on this, someone said, 'Why wouldn't she and she with none of her own?' And then someone else said, 'Hasn't she?' And they begin to nod and wink at each other, hinting at some dark relationship. Who knows, maybe one night long ago when the tide was high, some sailor had hove to at the riverside and by the time he had left, never to return, had made a happy home of it – for two!

The women predominated in another house on one of the lanes off Blarney Street. They were the Wilsons, a family of stunningly beautiful young men and women, each a milk-and-honeyed Adonis or Aphrodite in their way. It was a small low house with a single living-room which was always alive with the laughter of girls, while hair-curlers and nylons and bras were flung all over the place, to be hurriedly snapped up and shoved under the cushions when boyfriends came calling. The Wilson girls' big venue on weekend nights was St Mary's Hall at the top of Shandon Street or the Assembly Rooms downtown where, in the dark and gunsmoke commotion of Hopalong Cassidy and Buck Jones, the constricting bands of some of those bras would miraculously come loose to the touch of well-tutored hands.

In the midst of all this singing and dancing, of curlers and nylons and the shouts of women, would sit their father, Ned Wilson, handsome as Nelson Eddy, and his wife, better-looking and certainly better endowed than Jeanette MacDonald. He's in an armchair in the corner with the one leg he came away with from the Somme stretched out in front and the crutch by the fire on the other side. A monarch of all he surveyed he surely is then and, since there is nothing much he can do, his great big sunflower wife is happy enough with that. She is another of that ubiquitous band of fruit-and-vegetable dealers who, when the day's work is done, loads the baskets of her trade on her back and, the coins jingling in her apron-pockets, swags them up the hill to her throbbing moss-lined home. So she is matriarch, bread-winner and queen mother all in one; that is light-years before the notion of liberated women came to the fore.

So it was women, women, women all the way; the men, those who survived, being squeezed into incongruous corners and never coming out but for a few hours on Sunday when they went down town to swap old glories in the smoke and dust of the last pub between them and eternity.

If our own house wasn't much like that, it was more our mother's doing than our father's. She was hell-bent on our making it out of this dark underworld into the light of day –

which meant schools, books, homework – all the disciplines that would mark our course. Two brothers, Dickie and Danny Shortland, up the road from us, made it into the civil service, setting the pattern for us all. But it was a cold, unlit, dreary passage and anything that would help distract us from it was good.

A prime mover in this distraction was our sister Eily, twenty years older than me and long past schooling by the time I arrived. There was a good reason for this, one which would not have happened in later times.

One day when she was a little one of six, she slipped on the icy steps of the North Presentation Convent where she was at school and came tumbling down the whole flight. Months of surgery and years of hospital followed which, by the time it was all done, left her with one leg several inches shorter than the other. There was no question of damages or compensation in those years; or, if there was, it could not be taken against the holy nuns who, being Sisters of Charity, had enough to do with their charity in giving the penniless waifs of the North Side free education without having to provide for their upkeep as well. Besides which, Mother would never have taken a case against them: 'They're God's anointed; you'd have no luck.' Being an act of God, it had to be taken as such, incompetent and botched surgery and all. So we end up with an invalid, the eldest of our family, our father's 'sweet bird of youth', a sapphire shimmering in the starlight, her eyes forever alight with wonder. By the time I come to know her, she has this crippled leg and hops up and down on it like a maimed bird. She will be marked out by her disfigurement for the rest of her life.

For all the years before I arrived, Eily used crutches, but I have no memory at all of them. The story goes that she went to Lourdes on a pilgrimage with the Dominicans of Pope's Quay and one night, crying with pain from the injured leg, a lady all dressed in white came up the dormitory floor, touched her and said, 'You'll cry no more now, child'. Instantly, the pain was gone. What's more, so the story goes, when the pilgrimage sailed back home to Cork, she left the crutches behind her in Lourdes.

There are reputed to be hundreds of Lourdes miracles; who knows, maybe this was one of them? All I know is that by the time I come along, the crutches are no longer there; and Eily has this extraordinary attachment to the 'Enfant de Marie' Lourdes medal which she always wears and which in times of distress she will prayerfully clutch, invoking the lady in white to help her.

And distress there will be aplenty. Every so often the area around her damaged hip breaks out in huge carbuncular boils which, as they ripen, become angry and inflamed with a horrible yellow pus.

The treatment for this – oh God, the barbarity of times past! – is the application of steaming bread poultices, an unbearable torture which no creature, animal or human, could endure without screaming. The tension builds up around us as the time for this comes on: the bread steeped in the boiling pot and then taken out to be laid on the poultice cloth and brought upstairs before it cools off. Each and every step on that stairs is marked with scars upon my heart. One by one I will count them until our mother reaches the top. Then I stop breathing and try to stop my ears, but I can't because my sister's screams rip through my heart and tear me to pieces. How Mother, a woman of gigantic courage, can do it is beyond us, but she does and it works and the angry pustulous mounds begin to break and what's inside comes out and we can all live in peace and quiet again.

The next morning our sister will be back down in the middle of us, smiling and free as if nothing had happened. And it will go on like that until the next time, with the life of laughter and fun and music she makes around us starting up all over again.

Her injury meant that she could never really have a job, so the good Sisters had arranged long ago for her to do a course in dressmaking – which was fine, only we could never afford the price of a sewing-machine. When eventually we did manage to buy one – God be praised for the moneylenders! – the skill was still there and very soon she was much in demand. The sewing-machine was the centre of it, rattling away at all hours of the day and night; but, side by side with this, she became quite a hand at fortune-telling and in no time at all the word was out that she was a world-class expert!

For this, the teapot and cups would be placed on the table, a cup to each 'customer', girls mostly but older women too, all in quest of good news. When the tea was finished, she'd take the cups and swirl the tea-leaves round and round until they had settled in one place. Then the magic tidings were told: 'I see a lump sum of money'; 'There's a change for the better coming'; 'There's a man to the house'; 'I see a kindly stranger'; 'There'll be a long walk between trees and water. And at the end of it ...' – 'What, what?' – 'Yes, yes, I see a tall dark stranger.' At last, the final explosive revelation: 'I see a wedding-ring.'

Screams and shouts of jubilation follow, interspersed with hushed and crooning silences. Fairytales unfold, happy dreams come true. The agony and the ecstasy play side by side, and the agony of the bread poultices is forgotten, as the shilling and sixpenny fees alchemise into a happy hunting-ground in our penny-dreadful world.

I don't know if the sewing-machine ever made any money. Even if it did, as much and more went out again, with everyone who came staying on; the house was always full, mothers with daughters, sisters with pals, patterns, lengths and rolls of cloth, half-made coats and tacked-up dresses, costumes, curtains, cretonnes, organdies, silks, all waiting their turn on the clickety-clack machine, to be touched and turned by our crippled fairy-godmother into cloths of gold.

And then it's Maytime – with Nelson Eddy and Jeanette MacDonald singing their hearts out for 'Springtime, love-time, May' on Eily's cracked His Master's Voice records and a whole host of troubadours, male and female, backing them up – Gracie Fields, the new young star Vera Lynn, Richard Tauber, Peter Dawson, Paul Robeson, and John McCormack with 'Sweet Alice Benbolt', who must have died a thousand times while the love-and-fortunes game went on to the race and rhythm of the Singer clickety-clack.

And there were love affairs. These were exclusively with film stars – Errol Flynn, Tyrone Power, Franchot Tone, Gary Cooper, Clark Gable and Spencer Tracy. And, of course, the virgin-birth of them all – tall, blonde, and with the head of a Nordic God – Leslie Howard. Every time a film of his came to the Pavilion or the Savoy, the whole gaggle would troop off down and come back home afterwards, to lock themselves in the room and put the sewing-machine to one side, and listen all night long to wonderful new good fortunes about a tall blonde man coming into their lives!

It couldn't last. Aggie Munn, on one of her flying visits from Dagenham, brought the offer of a seamstress job for her in a local factory. The promise of real money every week instead of the fortune-telling/dressmaking shillings and pence was too much to turn down. 'Sure, won't she be back over for Christmas?' Aggie cunningly plied. 'Think of the style and grandeur she'll have to show off then!'

There's this party in the house the night before she leaves. It's a great night of singing and dancing; all the fortune-telling girls and women are there, though it's far too brash and noisy for the soulful company of Leslie Howard. But sooner or later it will end. It's a moment we all dread. After the crowd has gone, a neighbour woman comes to take away old clickety-clack, which she has bought 'to put a few shillings in the girl's pocket and she going away'. Up to that, the reality of her leaving has not struck us. But the sight of it going out the door brings the whole thing alive. Mother starts, then we're all at it. I fly upstairs to hide my head under a pillow where I won't be seen. None of us knew until that moment how much she has meant to us.

But our grief is short-lived. Within a year, she is back. Hitler's Luftwaffe had the air-raid sirens wailing over London, which would have been reason enough, but I like to think she came back because she couldn't bear being away from us any longer. And, wonder of wonders, back with her comes a brand-new sewing-machine, the price and profit of her London earnings.

So the whole rigmarole starts up again, the girls and women crowding in once more, the dress-making and the fortune-telling, His Master's Voice records bawling away on the crackly gramophone, and Leslie Howard bursting new upon the scene as the gorgeous Ashley Wilkes in 'Gone With the Wind'.

It is not the end of the story, but it is close enough to the end for me to be nearly able to finish it here. Yet not quite. Because, within the year, incredibly, Eily was married and gone from us for good. It wasn't Errol Flynn, or Clark Gable, or Gary Cooper, and sure to hell it wasn't the father, son and holy ghost of them all, the blonde godhead Leslie Howard.

But 'Fox' Bickerstaffe was a good man; they had children and a fair enough life together for a dozen or so years. We kept in close touch with her; we went to see her and she came to us, and the same brightness was always there.

But I leave all that now, to be remembered or forgotten like the flotsam and jetsam of all our lives, and jump ahead to the next time I fled from the sight of people to avoid being seen getting into a state about her. By then the injured leg did what it was always threatening to do: it became incurably tuberculous. The disease spread like a rip-tide through her; the bread-poultices and prayers to the White Lady of Lourdes were of no avail anymore.

I was well gone from home by now, but the maimed girl who had cradled me through my infant years and sang and danced her way through my growing ones was still there somewhere in the background, and in a few scrawled lines on a sheet torn from a school jotter, she told me she would go on like that now to the end:

The family are well including Daddy, except myself who am poorly enough this time. The time is long when you're in hospital, especially the likes of me who could never bear being locked up. Sometimes I think I'm gone entirely, and the nuns start saying Rosaries over me which puts me in the horrors altogether. The next thing I'll be seeing is big black tealeaves on the lip of my cup, which means a coffin – Bill, do you remember? But I'll be getting up for Easter when you're home. And the girls will come, and we'll sing all the old songs, and we'll have a great night, just like old times again.

I did come, but it wasn't she who was there before me but some changeling they had put in the bed in her place. Her face was gone; there was nothing but the big blue eyes fighting off the tears that sprang up at the sight of me.

I fled from the place as soon as I decently could, got out

into the clean air where there was no God, only the God of the living, the God of those who must go on after seeing such things and try to live without them. But the memory of her standing between chairs, holding herself erect upon uneven legs to dance the Blackbird Hornpipe, of the Singer clickety-clack going full belt at Christmas time when all the girls wanted new things, of the tea-leaves in the cups and the fortune-hopefuls all about her – all that will never go away, because it will never be like that, never again.

Her great pal, Madgie Murphy, led the troupe of girls as they walked beside her coffin down to St Patrick's Church. She would have liked that – the lipstick and rouge and stiletto heels, you could almost hear them singing as they went along:

The bells of hell go ting-a-ling-a-ling
For you but not for me;
Oh, death, where is thy sting-a-ling-a-ling
Or grave thy victory?

Close on 50 years have passed since then but Eily is still part of us. She is one of the few who have left marks and scars upon us and opened up pathways that have never since quite closed. From the memory of her wounded years, of the screams of pain that went straight to the marrow of my soul, to this day I can never bear the sight of pain in man or beast without trying to stop it. I will rescue a fly from a spider's web, will push a worm from being trampled on a footpath, will cut the stem of a flower, rather than see it die on the stalk. Once, out on a rabbit-shoot with a friend, on my first shot – I must have that 20/20 vision of my father – I hit a grazer 200 yards off and, thrilled with the shot (are we all killers by nature?) I ran up to find the little thing twitching in agony and there and then had three more shots at it to put it out of pain. And I have never taken a gun in my hands since. Some of my children have inherited the weakness, if that is what it is. On his first hunting exploit, one of the boys hooked a baby mackerel and came ashore to proudly show it off. But as it twitched on the line, he suddenly stopped, took the hook from its mouth and threw it back in the sea where, by now he said, its brothers and sisters would be out searching for it.

So I would be a poor hand at opposing euthanasia where there is great pain and would certainly favour potent drugs to relieve it. But I know too that there are things worse than physical pain: loneliness, the deprivation of the unloved, parting and separation from loved ones, which in its way is a kind of death. Those are the most inhumane killers of all.

And so it is that, through that frail and injured morsel of humanity who was a third mother to me through my early life, I became part of that broad sweep of living whose sources are everywhere because they are blood and bone of our imperilled life. But neither pain nor suffering nor deprivation nor death can ever stop the heart from loving; and in pain, suffering, deprivation and death from loving most of all.

I owe much of all this to my crippled sister, living out her life in an agony of contradictions. For her, when there was nothing else to hope for, she could at least be sure that she was held in the cocoon of our love. A love of which I, in my careless and inattentive way, was lucky to be a part. And, as she grew older and her own children were growing too, she would come back and back to us, finding in us a safe haven from an anguished, troubled life.

We put her to rest at last with our father, his first and dearest child, his 'sweet bird of youth'. Our mother and brothers are with her there now too – all together again as they had been long ago, long before I was reckoned on at all. But I am glad I was, if for no other reason than to be able to tell their story here and to say 'Thanks, it was so good to be one of you'.

8

'THE ANCHOR'S WEIGHED'

EMIGRATION, the constant of Irish life since the Famine of
'Black '47', continues down to our own day. The long history of conquest and the rape of native resources meant a continuing blood-letting, which inevitably got into the litera-
ture, most of it excruciatingly sad, and some – like the
Sawdoctors' popsong 'The N 17', the main route out of
Galway for the emigrant flight from Shannon to Boston or
New York – full of a savage but stoic resignation. Swinging
between the poles of anger and grief, both of which are helpless against the recurring plague, it becomes fertile soil for
parody, satire and a pitiless and mordant wit. The pain of
going away, of being away, of being left alone behind – these
are all part and parcel of our psyche, as common to us as the
air we breathe or the food we eat.

All our childhoods echo with the names of places we had
never seen: the Bronx, Brooklyn, Manhattan, Long Island,
Boston Common, Camden Town, the Ford Motor Works of
Dagenham and Detroit, the streets of Philadelphia. Our footprints on the sands of time are footprints on the pavements

of those places. Sisters, brothers, uncles and aunts, cousins, relatives, friends – the stamps and postmarks on their letters home are a coloured panoply of our emigrant lives. It was the story of our family and of all the other families up and down the road. The names 'Dagenham' and 'the Bronx' were far more often on our lips than any place in Ireland. The reason for this tells its own emigration story: the original Henry Ford came from the small village of Ballinascarty in West Cork which he left, like so many others of his time, to make a life for himself in the New World. But old loyalties remained and, in time, the name of Ford would come to Cork, at the time a God-given lift to the depressed economy. But there were always hiccups and halts and, when these happened, the Cork plant would go on short time or shut down and the Dagenham plant would take over.

Then, come Christmas, and hordes of 'Ford' emigrants – 'Dagenham Yanks' we called them – would be back, like some latter-day influx of 'boat people' or Puerto Rican stowaways, only this influx had money to burn. There we'd be, the rest of us, marooned on the shores of dole-ridden Cork, while they flashed wads of sterling notes, turning our heads to the glittering prizes that awaited us if only we had the gumption to get up and go to the far side.

What Christmases of 'eat, drink and be merry' they were for them then, as up and down the road they went, peacocks in fawn crombies and white silk scarves – the spivs and beatniks of a later time but, boy oh boy, what paragons of fashion they seemed to us! Tommy Walsh, whose only labour before he went to Dagenham was the Labour Exchange, never missed the chance of showing off as he passed our door, shaking his glittering prize of a flashy wrist-watch, putting it up to his ear, ostensibly to see if it's still ticking but really to let us all know that he has one, to let us know too that the great ambition of upwardly mobile mothers, like our own, to turn their sons into nice white-collar civil servants, complete with pension and permanence, was so much bullshit compared to the rich fleshpots of Dagenham and Camden Town.

So the Dagenhams and Camden Towns, the Birminghams and Boston Commons figured a lot more in our global map than did the uncharted city of Dublin, headquarters of that civil service all good mothers dreamed about and capital of our new-found State. A postulant for fame in the civil service in Dublin had to be instructed in the wiles and ways of his own capital city, whereas one going to far foreign fields in those places did not. There were hundreds of his own kind there before him who were ready and willing to give him a helping hand. Certainly, no one ever went to the States without someone on the far side to look after him. Years later, when that particular outflow was down to a trickle, a good friend (Richard Power, author of a fine novel, *The Hungry Grass*) was going out on a creative writing fellowship when a cousin who happened to be home on holiday heard about him. 'Who's meeting him?' he asked and, when told no one was, he exploded. 'Jeez, the kid can't do that. No one goes to New York without someone to meet them. He could get into all sorts of scrapes in a place like that. Get me his flight number and his arrival time and I'll see he's looked after.'

Local boy makes good had a long way to go before he could ever come to anything at home, but local boys made good in that El Dorado all the time. Never a word was said about the bad side, about the drunks and down-and-outs, the breadline bums and the subway sleepers – that would make nonsense of the faraway hills being green, which by definition they always were. True or false, it was the dream outlet for the destitute millions who down through the years had fled the ill-fared land to find fame and fortune where so many of their kind had found it before.

And when John F. Kennedy came to Ireland five months before his death to remind us that for the long generations of Irish emigrants the Atlantic was 'that bowl of bitter tears', we all knew in our hearts what he meant.

Like Connie Conroy's mother who ran down the road after him the day he went away, wailing like a mad woman, 'Come back, come back. I'll die if you go away!' And the neighbours gathered round her and held her, each knowing in her own life exactly what she meant. So the foolish boy puts his suitcase down and comes back and they cling to each other until nothing will get them apart, but something does – a sundering so grievous that nothing in life or death will ever again be able to heal.

As for Connie, what he's thinking at that moment is something like: this bleak unlovely place, this drab grey ribbon of houses, the pinchpenny neighbours with pinchpenny lives – why should I ever want to stay here, why should I ever want to come back? I dreamed and dreamed of this day, the day when at last I got up and got out, and now it's here and the heart is coming apart inside me and I can't stand the sight of her face all red and wet with tears! Just shove her off, someone, and get me the hell away from here, get her and it and everything to do with it out of my life and memory forever. If I do what she's saying and stay, I'm an oil-rag toady on the footplate of a train-engine for the rest of my days, just like my father before me. He never got the chance I'm getting, or maybe he did and didn't take it, so get up and get out; the skyscrapers of Manhattan are calling – they can be my footplate now, if only this woman will stop wailing and let me go.

He takes one last look up the road; it's as dull and grey as it always was, but it's the only road and they are the only people in the world he will ever call his own. So he grabs the suitcase and turns his back on it and them and will not turn again, for if he does he's like Lot's wife, turned into a pillar of salt – a just judgement on a soul too weak for the bright new world that awaits him. And as he passes The Mountain pub on Evergreen, he looks in and sees the clouds of cigarette-smoke through the fogged-up windows and the Guinness flat in the pint glasses. And in that brief access of reality, he knows he's doing right, that the hopes and dreams of so many others died there, swallowed down through years of idleness with the same flat porter which became the only bright light in their lives.

Good transport and communications would put paid to all that and for the most part today's emigrants find the whole thing morbid and ridiculous. They come and go as they please; here today gone tomorrow, a quick phone-call to say we've arrived and are settling in and everything is OK. Even in the backwoods days, there was still the odd realist who shook off 'Ireland Mother Ireland' like water from a duck's back and got on with the day's living. Aggie Munn was such a one, who on her an-nual visit home from Dagenham would prance up and down the floor in her finery, telling our sister to 'shut off that ould ullagoaning' of John McCormack on His Master's Voice and give her something lively she could dance to. Whether we do or not, up she gets and starts jiving away in her fishnet stockings and stiletto heels, a crazy teenager high on drugs or worse, while Mother sits there frozen with disapproval. The false gods of pagan England will surely never take root in her house!

It is all part of our Irish blood-letting. From one day to the next, we never know who will be gone. Sometimes it isn't just one, it's whole families, sailing down the Lee on the *Innisfallen* with the dropping tide.

Paddy Kelly lives up the road from us, big brother Jim's great pal. When it comes to 'howlin' and fightin'', you can hear the roars of him halfway across town. Then suddenly the roaring stops and he's gone. The British Army takes him. Tuberculosis and the foundries of Coventry and Birmingham take the rest, until in the end not a single one is left but the old couple, moping about in a half-trance that springs to life only when one of them comes home. And they come too: the girls trailing stunned and befuddled young Englishmen behind them, blue-eyed boys in Burtons suits and with 'twangs' you can cut with a knife. The real triumph is in their names: not Murphy or Buckley or Sullivan or any home-grown stuff, but Meddlicott, Fraipe, Chalmers, names as rich and enchanting as the minted herbs of Araby.

They are part of the 'Dagenham Yanks' emigration stream; when the real Yanks come, what a sight they are: box-plaid trousers and caps to match, flowery shirts and technicolour coats, with five-, ten-, twenty-dollar bills stuffed into every pocket. A postcard on the mantelpiece of Nanny Apples' little hovel showed one of them, hot from the Ford Motor Works of Detroit, sitting behind the wheel of a gleaming new 'Fair Lane'. 'I often said I'd never die nor leave the world till I'd drive up Shandon Street in one of these,' the message says. 'Well, Nanny, it's very often I do be in one now.'

Such cards and letters, even more so what went with them, the 'emigrants' remittances', were the mainstay of our hopes and our economies. When the postman did his last round on Christmas Eve and there was no letter with an

American stamp and postmark, it was the death of all Christmas cheer. Nor was that only in our life in Cork. Years later, I met a man with the fine resounding name of MacDara O'Flaherty on the *Naomh Éanna* sailing out from Galway to the Aran Islands; he was an old chap who had spent his working life with the Boston Gas Company and was coming home for the first time in 50 years. His sisters were there on the quayside waiting for him, bent and withered crones, crippled with arthritis from the damp and misty air.

Their grief was palpable as they clung to each other, moaning the little words and names of their childhood in the Irish language, which meant that most of the other visitors around had no idea what they were saying, least of all his big Yankee son – a baseball giant in a tweed cap and suede coat, wondering to God what all the moaning and groaning was about! Was this the Ireland the ould fella kept filling him up with back home? This coven of witches under a weeping sky, the tears and rain pouring down in bucketfuls, as if there wasn't enough water about already?

Where was all the celebration – the gaiety, the songs and ballads, the dancing at the crossroads, the fiery if illegal poitín to put the heart in them – where was all that now? 'I'm getting the hell outa here as quick as I settle the old guy,' he tells me. 'Any chance of seeing one of the big games in Croke Park?'

And when the coven of crones moves to the pub on the pierhead, the old guy keeps plunging in and out of them, hugging them, holding them, clinging onto them till death do us part. And singing in a cracked and choking voice:

Take my blessing down to Connaught
For it is a wholesome place.

As if all that's not enough, isn't there this stranger on

holiday in Aran who gets so worked up by all the 'ullagoan-ing' that he chips in with his own haporth, a song which has nothing at all to do with them in this part of Ireland, but with another of the lost generations of Irishry: the Presbyterian smallholders of Ulster, who crossed the Atlantic in their thousands, forced to emigrate long before there was a whisper of a Great Famine at all:

> It was not for the want of employment at home
> That made the poor sons of Erin to roam;
> But the rents were getting higher and we could no longer pay,
> So farewell unto you, bonny, bonny Slieve Gallion Brae.

The baseball hero in the tweed cap is way out of his depth now. What's more, he doesn't drink – is that some stray by-product of the New England prohibitionist past, because sure as hell it's not from the old man he takes it! What with that and the language they're speaking – to him nothing but an aborigine gibberish – he can't get out of there fast enough. The last I see of him he's heading off down the road to the pierhead at Kilronan, the tweed cap sodden wet and the suede coat streaming, angrily asking what time the return boat leaves for Galway. For him, the fair hills of Ireland can be ten times fairer; thanks but no thanks. By now he's had more than his fill of them.

Judged by the standards of this time, the familial loyalty of those early generations of emigrants was indeed remarkable. The purpose of their going was often less to make a life for themselves than to pave the way for others to follow. One fare was enough to start a whole family, the first sending the fare back for the next and so on down the line. A Buckley cousin on Pope's Quay used the same cache of gold sovereigns to get others across the Atlantic five or six times after himself; another, now grown to a dynasty fifty, sixty times the strength, proudly boasts that when he sailed past the Statue of Liberty for the first time, he had the whole of his vast inheritance from Shandon Street with him: seventeen shillings in his pocket – and six hurleys!

There was a downside to all this familial faith, for if someone betrayed it, he or she was excised from tribal memory. They never sent home as much as 'the scrawl of a pin [pen]'. Such a one was Seamus Beck, an Oliver Reed with a wild rude energy, the heart and soul of the local Celtic soccer team; he went down the quays one night to see the *Innisfallen* out and, when his name was called for the first eleven the following Sunday, he was nowhere to be found. No one knew where he had gone to or how he had found the fare, or if indeed he went on the *Innisfallen* at all. He had just gone, vanished; we never heard of him again. The Noonan brothers were soccer players – two of them later became Irish internationals – until Paddy, the youngest, took the same route, hotly pursued by a policeman who was after him for some minor offence. He was lucky enough to have a pal on board the ship who fixed him up. The next we see or hear of him is years later when he comes home in the last stages of T.B., having lived rough in England ever since leaving.

Those were the bad stories, the 'Noreen Bawns', hell-bent on preaching the evils of emigration, as if for most of them there was any other option:

> There's a graveyard in Tirconnell where the flowers wildly
> wave,
> There's a grey-haired mother kneeling at a green and lonely
> grave;
> 'Ah, my Noreen,' she is saying, 'it's been lonely since you've
> gone,
> 'Twas the curse of emigration that lost me my Noreen Bawn.'

Now fond youths and tender maidens, ponder well before go
From your humble home in Ireland, what's beyond you'll
     never know.
What is gold and what is silver when your health and strength
     are gone?
When you think of emigration, please remember Noreen
     Bawn.

The emigrant prototype was always like that: young, handsome, the flower of the flock. Small wonder that, when they did go, it was indeed a kind of death; the phrase 'American Wake' tells the whole story: drinking, singing, dancing till the first light streaked the eastern sky. Then it was time to leave for the *Innisfallen* on the quays or, farther down, to Cove for the outbound liner to New York. It's a moment engraved forever on many memories: a page torn from a school jotter on which a neighbour writes the name and address of a relative out there brings back memories of the emigrant's schooldays; a torn jersey stuffed under a cushion tells of great feats on the hurling or football field; a long-forgotten photograph tossed away at the back of a drawer falls out with diabolic connivance as a mother fumbles for a clothes-brush to give a last lick to her departing boy. Then it's all over, the door is shut, and life, some sort of life, goes on. But never again the life together they had known.

Our cousin, Phil Buckley, was the first to go to the States. Predictably, he was ever after the golden boy, the flower of the flock. All the superlatives were lavished on him: he was strong, handsome, brave, a litany of traits and virtues calculated to iconise him into the family saint and, at the very least, an object most worthy of our young hero-worship. His brothers and sisters followed, helped as always by the pathfinder's dollars home. They all set up in the Bronx, a home from home each summer Sunday as they gathered in the hot and dusty confines of John Kerry O'Donnell's Gaelic Park, to follow the fortunes of the hurling and football emigrant teams. And, more relevant, to hear how Cork were doing back home, especially Glen Rovers, the North Side heroes from out the road in Blackpool. For the space of a few hours then, the Bronx became a microcosm of a lost life, a centre of gravity for hearts and minds gone astray like playboys of the western world.

And in the pubs and cafés afterwards, the tones and accents were the very same as those you'd hear in 'Hallo's' or 'Curry's' on Shandon Street, while the talk was all about hurling, bowl-playing, drag-hunting, the Glen, the Barrs, the Fair Hill Harriers, Tiger Aherne and Joulter Murray, champion bowl-players out Dublin Hill or 'lofting' the Viaduct on the Bandon Road on Sunday mornings – signs and sounds of a vast multitude of displaced persons, each a mini-Odysseus in his own right, gone long and far from the confines of his native place.

Phil Buckley did well, as the phrase goes, with a whole dynasty of attorneys and doctors and business-folk grown up around him; but not everyone had the same story. It took a later, more realistic, generation to tell us about the navvies who built the roads and railroads, the dockers slogging it out in racial battles on the waterfront, the hobos and down-and-outs picking the trash-bins or sidling up to the free-meals counter bumming their way from drink to drink with sob-stories about their hard luck and 'Buddy, can you spare a dime?'

But they weren't our emigrants, our local boys. Our boys lived in fabulous houses in places with fabulous names – Martha's Vineyard, Montawk, Huntington Long Island, places where golden lads and girls all must like fairy princes thrive or bust! Volleyball on the golden strands, gorgeous suntans, technicolour bikinis and shorts, iced shandies on the sprinkler lawns!

Much of it was fantasy, yet there was more than a grain of truth in it too, the chasm of difference between the life they lived and the life their elders had left behind, certainly more than they could ever understand.

When Phil came home for the first time in the 1960s, he fled from Dublin where he wanted to see one of the big games, swearing that 'the goddam place is too big, too complicated for me. I'm getting the hell out of here to some place I know'. So back down to 'where he knows' he goes, to spend his days walking about the streets of Cork, in and out of the lanes and alleyways, hanging over the river wall at Pope's Quay and listening to the sound of the Shandon bells, sounds and echoes he had dreamed about all the years he was away.

So he's caught both ways now: when he's away, he wants to be at home; when he's at home, he wants to be away. Is there any place right for him at all? And when he gets back, his daughters will be waiting for him at Kennedy airport, to pick him up in the big Fair Lane – that place in Cork city where the original Henry Ford's family lived when they came in from Ballinascarty. And they'll whisk him out across the Throg's Neck Bridge to Southport Long Island. Now that he's retired and has his family reared, I ask, would he not consider packing it all in and coming back? Not a chance, he says, there's too much water gone under the bridge; it would hurt the other way round now. The overhead railway in the Bronx, the white yachts scudding across the inlet at Southport, the manicured lawns of Huntington –

they're now home to him. So it's two worlds, the one now and the one then; and he's pincered between them, like some lost bird caught between rocks on a strange ledge, knowing it can be home only if he can wipe his memory clean and pretend there never was any other place.

Then, one year, I'm out there making one of my television talk-shows for transmission back in Ireland. There's a great gathering of the clans to greet me: the Buckleys, the Toolans, the Duffys, the Bacons, as well as Mazzurellis, Cherrys and other assorted mixtures – what the colonial Kipling would undoubtedly call 'lesser breeds without the law'! There's no fear Ireland will be forgotten! The songs Phil Buckley wants to hear are the Cork ones: 'The Banks of My Own Lovely Lee', 'Carrigdown', 'The Bells of Shandon'; the songs of emigration, 'Kathleen Mavourneen', 'Noreen Bawn', 'The Emi-grant's Farewell', can wait. Maybe by then he has come to the view that once is enough to endure such masochistic wounding. Nothing ages quicker than nostalgia. When we get to making the show itself, something remarkable happens. We're coming up towards the end with only a few minutes left when, not expecting too ardent a response – television audiences when put on the spot, can be notably reticent – I decide to take a chance and invite them to send greetings back home to their folks in Ireland.

There is a moment of silence, then the whole studio erupts, with everyone in the place trying to get in. It needs quick thinking on all sides but we manage it. We line them up in rows in front, facing the cameras; then one by one they come forward.

Suddenly, it's all there, the vast diaspora of the Irish in the world calling back to the little towns and villages of their childhood, places from a dim and distant past, a hinterland peopled by the living and the dead but, living or dead, still vivid in the mind and memory of the displaced Irish everywhere.

Much of the greater part of that diaspora started out from what was once Queenstown, now Cove. It's less than twenty miles downriver from us, yet in terms of what it meant in Irish life it's an eternity away. The names are still there on the seafront – the Manhattan Bar, the Atlantic Hotel – names and places that would come to mean more to those who went away than those left behind. There's a fine heritage centre there now telling the story of the exodus, with pictures showing the crowds waving goodbye as the tenders ferried them out to the liners at anchor in the sheltered bay. Whether it was drink, an ethnic melancholy or some darker Celtic trait in love with self-affliction, there was always someone on hand to sing the parting songs: 'The anchor's weighed, farewell, farewell' was a great favourite; when it was some boy or girl in the throes of young love who was leaving, this was the tearful *coup-de-grâce* that finished them off:

> Oh, angel of heaven, look down, guard and guide thee,
> Protect thee from evil, why can'st thou not be my own?
> Oh, stay but one moment, oh stay but one moment,
> One moment of ecstasy, thy heart throbbing on my breast;
> Life's long dream is o'er, life's dream is o'er,
> Farewell, farewell.

Consciously or otherwise, something of this must have got into the racial bloodstream – or maybe it wa s genuinely that such a sundering moment could never again be forgotten. Whatever the cause, it so happens that I come to have a very personal reason to be aware of it. It happened during the lecture circuits I did in the United States a few years back.

The theme was 'Flight Patterns' – four waves of

emigration from Ireland, with the songs, music and poetry associated with them: the Missionary Monks of the sixth and seventh centuries; the 'Flight of the Earls', O'Neill and O'Donnell, to Spain and Rome in the seventeenth; the 'Wild Geese' under Patrick Sarsfield, who fled to Europe following the defeat of the Catholic King James by the Protestant King Billy – source of all our troubles up North to this day; and, finally, the Great Famine of 1847 with the blood-letting that followed – half the eight million population either dead from hunger or fled across the Atlantic, often in what were known as 'coffin-ships'.

It was that final section of the show which really struck home. In quite large halls, with audiences of hundreds, you could feel the silence when it came to the poems and stories: the cottier who, on the night his children die in the Macroom Workhouse, carries his starving wife on his back to their empty hovel, where there is now no hope left; and the following morning, the neighbours find them both dead, her frozen feet inside his tattered báinín shirt. Or the little girl in Knocknafulla in south Tipperary, the sole survivor of a family which has perished, who brings it all back years later with a poem in Irish, the only language she knows:

> *Is iad na prátaí dubha a d'fhág ár muintir treascartha,*
> *A chuir ins an 'Poorhouse' iad is anonn thar farraige –*

> It was the blackened potatoes that ruined our people,
> Sent them to Poorhouses and across the wave;
> And the hillside graveyard saw the last of hordes of them –
> Oh, God of pity, could you not save?

> The starving Irish stricken with misery
> Go down in anguish with the pain of death;the young cry out
> – 'Oh, please, please pity me,
> Ease from this hunger we'll never get.'

Working out of a single spotlight, I would occasionally look out beyond the light to the audience in the tiered seats ahead. And never once in all those twenty cities – north, south, east, west – never once did I not catch a glimpse of the tears being wiped away, a secret sign of communal grief. And those were not the children of the Famine Time which was a 150 years before, but those of cousin Phil Buckley's time and later, four, five, six generations on.

There is a final twist to Phil's story, as macabre and ironic as it is sad. Having spent a lifetime with the Ford Motor Company – first in Cork, then Detroit, then New York – he could never bring himself to drive any but a Ford car. There is an even older loyalty than the job: hadn't the first Henry Ford lived in the same place as himself before going to the States, hence the glamorous 'Fair Lane' which, though now retired and well beyond his needs, he had just bought. But old habits die hard and nothing will stop the former foreman from lifting the bonnet to see if they make them as good now as they did in his day. Well, curiosity killed the cat – as it will surely kill him: the holding-lever slips, the bonnet comes crashing down, a stunning blow to the back of his head which would certainly have killed anyone else there and then, but like that old Nanny Apples grandmother of ours long ago, Phil just shakes himself and walks away. And that should be the end of it. But 'Fair Lane' has the last laugh.

Back home for a last hurrah in Cork, he begins to have dizzy spells; then, at a hurling match in which his beloved Glen Rovers are playing, he gets so worked up that he falls down in a fainting fit and has to be brought to hospital. There's a brain-scan, the news is bad, he is given something to tide him over until he gets back to America.

On the tarmac at Shannon where we go to see him off, he waves a last goodbye. It's not 'The Anchor's Weighed' this time, that's all of 50 years ago; it's the Boeing 747 now. Off he goes but he's hardly arrived when he's brought to hospital again – only this time it's for good. He dies on New Year's Day – 60 years to the day after he first left.

In the cemetery in Huntington, Long Island where he is buried, there is no shortage of Irish names. He should be as much at home there as in the Curraghkippane above the banks of his own lovely Lee where his grandmother, Nanny Apples, and all his people before him are. But is he? I doubt it. Like all those displaced persons of our Irish past, at the very least he would have a problem making up his mind. Alive, he could never seem to be clear where home was for him anymore. The seventeen shillings he brought out with him became the million dollar bills he and his have made since; and the six hurleys, relics of his glory-days with 'The Glen', became the baseball bats of a generation of clean new American boys. Of course he loved them as any father and grandfather would. But, in the midst of the big open-plan houses and the fine sprinkler lawns, there is something always missing: the call of the wild from the green fields beyond Blackpool and the even more piercing call from the warren of lanes around Shandon Street and Bachelors' Quay. That will be with him and the likes of him forever: a familiar world gone down with the last light and a strange one coming up with the new light rising. Caught there between them, he is an island of grief and loneliness, forever hoping for a life of some new world to come.

9

THOSE WERE THE DAYS, MY FRIENDS

No doubt you will have the impression by now that what I am writing here is a sad book and in ways I am. You couldn't have lived in that place at that time and write anything else. Yet there is another side to it. A hilarious and jovial one, with singing, dancing and carousing into the small hours. Anyone who could sing was welcome; anyone who could harmonise was doubly so. That meant an even more total involvement, the sound being enough without any words to get the whole crowd in. Indeed the words were sometimes made up as we went along – any old words would do so long as they filled the lines. So for 'Twas said that Cromwell hanged them, the black and bitter crew' in John McCormack's 'Fairy Tree', we sang a more reverential paean to the Lord Protector: 'Twas said that Cromwell hanged them, the black and bitter hoor.' 'Kelly the boy from Killane' got mixed up with 'Hail Glorious Saint Patrick' in a fine description of his manly frame: 'Seven feet was his height to the mansions above.' And La Marseillaise, the French National Anthem, went off to a great rousing chorus:

'Ye sons of France, ye hoors, ye gets.' The fat woman in the rowing boat shouting at her husband to 'Sing, Henry, like the gondolas do', made excellent good sense to us since, if the gondolas could sing, then by all means let them; everyone else did! A neighbour's prowess was often measured by how well he could lead a crowd in a chorus at a party or in a pub, though the singing happened in all sorts of other places as well.

In our wide and varied family circle, there was only one member who did not sing; that was Father's brother, Uncle Timmy, a stolid man with a face of granite, out of which shone two large bluebell eyes. This was so exceptional that it had to have some explanation. One story was that it was something to do with what had happened in the war. According to this story, he is lying shell-shocked in the mud of No-Man's-Land, with the dead and dying about him, when a German scouting patrol comes past, bayoneting anyone still showing signs of life.

Timmy realises that his sole chance of survival is to act so dead that they won't bother with him – a feat of such rigid concentration that it burnt a frozen pose upon him for the rest of his life. But it doesn't stop there. As the scouting patrol goes past, one of them strikes out at his bandolier with his bayonet, slashing a cut a foot long across his stomach. Being 'dead', he cannot now suddenly come to life because that will certainly be the end of him. So, by a prodigious feat of control, he chokes the gasp of pain and stays dead – and lives to tell the tale.

Later, he becomes a prisoner of war and is locked up with his pipe and his silences for the duration. And when it is all over, he is sent back home safe and sound and has a pension which, though small, can keep him in silent, if frugal, comfort for the rest of his life.

As ill-luck will have it, that pension is bigger than Father's, a disparity which rankles, especially with someone who has endured 'the burden of the day and the heats'. Though brothers, you really would wonder how two such glaringly contradic-tory spirits could come out of the same house. This difference will come to a head on Christmas nights when Mother, always strong on family loyalty, will insist that her fiery particle of a man go over to bring his only brother back for the festive singing and carousing. Father grumbles a bit but eventually goes and, either from boredom or loneliness on the holy night, some remote chord of affection will be touched in our uncle by the sight of his mercurial brother coming to take him away from the loneliness of his little paraffin-lit room. Not alone will he always come but, with the company about him, he will be moved miraculously, not to song – never that! – but to stories; again, as ill-luck will have it, to stories which turn upon the one topic that is taboo as far as Father is concerned: the bloody war! The pace of Timmy's speech is such that the Hundred Years War itself would be over by the time he's finished; meanwhile, we all sit around and listen as he drones on. 'We were in Fraaance ... it was the dead of night ... and I was on sentry-go-o-o.' We have heard it all before, the same story, the same drone, the same mindless boredom. We'd be asleep if we could but we can't; the noise keeps us awake. All this time, Father is getting angrier and angrier. He's swallowing his Guinness in short sharp gulps, which he hopes will hurry things on, but they don't; they only slow them down.

Mother, who is used to the scene, sees that Father's fuse is burning, so she's doing her best to edge Timmy along, pushing fresh bottles of stout under his nose to see if that will help, but it doesn't. At last, the fuse-wire runs out and Father explodes. 'What in the name of Christ war are you talking about? What war did you ever see that got yourself locked up safe and sound in a prisoner-of-war camp for three years and nine months and left poor hoors like me to do the fighting?' And then the final insult: 'And what's more, come home to fine fat pensions afterwards.'

Oh, the fat is in the fire now! In one of the rare rapid movements of his life, Timmy is up and away and Mother starts bawling at them: 'For Jesus, Mary and Joseph's sake, will ye not keep the peace on the holy and blessed night? Sit down, sit down, Timmy, he don't mean it. Don't walk out the door on us and make a show of us before the neighbours. Kenny don't mean it. He has a few drinks taken; he'll be better in the morning.'

That's the final stroke and drives Father wild entirely. The idea that it's his fault, that it's the drink and not the stupid bloody story which he has heard a hundred times that has caused him finally to blow, is more than he can take. He throws Timmy's cap after him and makes to go up to bed himself, a catastrophic rift that will surely never be healed. Mother sees that there's only one way now to head off the disaster – and that's with singing. Because, dumb as he is, and cut to the quick now too by this latest affront, our uncle loves to hear us singing. From the loneliness of his own little hovel on Drummy's Lawn off Shandon Street, we must sound like the angels singing 'Adeste' from heaven. Just to be there with us, listening to us harmonising, and him there in the midst of us, is more than he can resist. So we start up urgently at Mother's request. And what a contrast the song we sing is to the scene we have just witnessed!

Oh, of all places the wide world around,
Home is the best, dearest home.
Happier spot have our feet never found,
Home is the best, dearest home.

Father and mother make holy the place,
Sisters and brothers adorn it with grace,
Gentle affection illumines each face,
Home is the best, dearest home.

Timmy will settle down then and later go home, content to spend another year of isolation, with the only singing he'll hear the chirping of the linnet in the bird-cage which he keeps hanging under the eave for company.

The same linnet is the closest thing in the world to him. When he takes the cage down from its hook at night, he brings it in, shuts the door behind him, opens the tiny cage-door and lets the little bird out to fly. Away it goes then, chirping and twittering in the cluttered room until, at last, it alights on the peak of his cap, where the old man has cunningly set some birdseed. He'll talk to it then and it will answer: a two-way traffic in total communication for which love is the conduit. Years later, I will write a story about that, 'Partners in Solitude' – the lone man and the caged linnet let out for a while to play about him. But then one night he forgets to shut the front door after he brings in the cage, the linnet gets out and flies away and, night by night after that, he's out there standing at the door and looking up at the roofs and gables, wondering which of all the birds up there is his. He pines away without his little companion and dies – but not before giving the neighbours who come to look after him strict instructions about what they're to do:

'When I'm gone, neighbours,' he tells them, 'I want ye to promise me wan thing!'

'What's that?' they ask.

'I want ye to promise that when I'm gone, ye'll not forget to water the linnet.'

It's like a dream to me that I seem to remember visiting Uncle Timmy during his last days. He is sitting up in the bed looking about him for someone to come or something to happen which will engage his attention.

But nothing does. There is a silence about him which has been there all his life, a 'Waiting for Godot' who never comes – certainly since that terrible day in the trenches long before when the silence was riven with the cries and agony of dying men all around him; and, later, in the years that followed in the prisoner-of-war camp, where only some deep and canny sense of self-composure derived from God-knows-what hidden source of strength helped to keep him sane.

In this dream, or whatever it is, his bluebell eyes come alive with pleasure at the sight of me and there is delight in his voice as he puts out his hands in greeting. It is an unaccustomed response from someone who has always been so remote. When I think hard about it, I know it did not happen, but the imprint is strong; even if it is only in my imagination that it exists, it is just as real as if it were true: a wishful thinking for a coming together which did not nor ever could take place, except in some disembodied world where the spirit subsists beneath the flesh and the reality is so much more than the dull corporeal world in which we live.

In that imagined scene I become another William Murphy, his father's name. But I am his brother's son, that old father's grandson – yet at that moment all three of us become one, a single undivided moment, a moment snatched from eternity. His greeting, his eyes, his hands reaching out to me, my own coming towards him – they are the still-frame of our whole existence, a single seamless unit of inter-connectability with nothing divided or separate about any of us anymore. It is a moment of tolerance, forgiveness and mutual understanding. The deadly drone of his voice and speech on Christmas nights, our own deadly boredom with him, our father's fury, our mother's distracted pleading – all these are superficial etchings upon the wider scene, their harsh unlovely edges blurred to nothing, with only the essence of us remaining.

It is a crazy dream. I would dearly love for it to have happened, but I know it did not. If it had, it would tell me we had not betrayed him after all, that our father's anger was not anger but a kind of love in its way, turned upside down. And that our mother had the right of it when she insisted that he be there in the midst of us 'on the holy and blessed night'.

And Timmy himself, living out his life in the little low-eaved hovel in Drummy's Lawn, where does he fit in the picture? That he was not the lost and isolated soul he must have thought himself, with nothing but a caged bird to thank him for being alive, but was instead a part of us as we were part of him. Sometimes I find myself praying that the dream really happened. At such times I am with the poet, Edward Thomas, in that express-train in the silence of 'Adlestrop', caught in that same still-frame moment, when we become new-minted creatures in a glory exclusively our own:

Yes. I remember Adlestrop –
The name, because one afternoon
Of heat the express-train drew up there
Unwontedly. It was late June.

The steam hissed. Someone cleared his throat.
No one left and no one came
On the bare platform. What I saw
Was Adlestrop – only the name

And willows, willow-herb, and grass,
And meadowsweet, and haycocks dry,

No whit less still and lonely fair
Than the high cloudlets in the sky.

And for that minute a blackbird sang
Close by, and round him, mistier,
Farther and farther, all the birds
Of Oxfordshire and Gloucestershire.

Two other uncles, Mother's brothers, Johnny and
Thomas, revolted against the puritan disciplines of their
self-righteous father and took the first chance they got to
escape. The only option then available was the British
Army. Fortunately for them, Mother England in those days
seemed to be always at war. The 'separation money' regularly in the post would keep the home fires burning. And
the womenfolk would do what the old song said: 'Turn the
dark cloud inside out, till the boys come home.'

My lasting memory of Uncle Johnny is of a man on
crutches with an empty trouser-leg; the leg that should be
there had been left behind on the silver sands of the
Bosphorus during the slaughter of the Dardanelles in
1915, when the Munsters became cannon-fodder for the
great Sir Ian Hamilton, surely a prototype for Siegfried
Sassoon's 'scarlet Majors at the base' who, 'when the war
is done and youth stone dead', would 'toddle safely home
and die – in bed'.

His wife, that Aggie Munn of the fur coats and stiletto
heels, fled from him and the bleak and squalid lanes of Cork
to make a new life for herself amongst the Irish in London.
There, she ran a highly lucrative boarding-house, never short
of lodgers in the home-from-home of Dagenham at that time.
Johnny, landed back with his own mother, our Nanny
Apples, years after he left her, was now no longer the wild
and wilful boy his righteous father had failed to intimidate,

147

but a broken angry man, a one-legged 'Johnny-I-hardly-knew-ye' – with no more waltzing, Matilda, for him! Mother loved him, as indeed did all the family; he had once been eldest son, flower of the flock and the cherished hope of their house. Now, here he was, ageing and beaten, his wife gone, his children too, back where he started. Only he's not the flower of the flock anymore but a lopsided scarecrow on a peg-leg, glad of the scraps of human kindness that come his way. These are the mudflats of despair on which his ill-starred odyssey has fetched him up.

He is the first dead person I will ever consciously kiss! I jest not and this is not some crazy necrophilia, for I am five and do not know what kissing is about. But such is the familial love that surrounds our Uncle Johnny that we are all brought along by Mother to kiss him goodbye. I remember the stone-cold feel of his forehead; no longer man, nor anything human, but something flat and dead – very, very dead, which my Uncle Johnny certainly never was before.

I must have had a good look at him then because his face will be imprinted forever on my mind. And fully half a century later, in the arrivals lounge of La Guardia Airport in New York it is suddenly there before me again in the person of his son, my cousin Phil Buckley: the same broad face, flat nose and furrowed forehead. 'Can these bones live?' asks the prophet Ezekiel. And yes, yes, is the answer.

.

Mother's second brother, our Uncle Thomas, was an even more shadowy figure than Johnny; he had departed the scene long before I arrived. He was the one our father met in the line marching up from Rouen at the start of the Great War, coughing his lungs up but still anxious to see a bit of action before he gave in. Father, the more seasoned soldier and by now disillusioned with jingoistic rantings about King and Country and the glories of Empire, took him to one side and told him to get to hell out of there back home before the cough, not the Germans, got him. The Regimental Medic, when he did find him, saw at a glance what any fool could see: that he was well on his way with TB and would comfortably make it to death's door without the grace and favour of any Bren-guns to help him. What was more crucial to the Munster Fusilier's cause was that, if left there, he could infect half the regiment as well as himself; so in short order he's put on the sick-list, then shipped home and spends the rest of his days in the sick bay of Tipperary Military Barracks, where he can sing 'It's a long way to Tipperary' for all he's worth because there won't be any more going back to war for him. For this, in due course, his widow, our Mamie Lane, is rewarded with that full pension of twenty-six and eight pence a week – a good and wholesome recompense for the single boat-trip to Boulogne which her unhappy warrior made. Father always felt that that was one case where His Majesty's Ministry of Pensions did not get the better of them.

So we come at last to our Uncle Jimmy, the only one of our mother's three brothers we knew at all well. He was without doubt the odd-man-out amongst them, not just being the youngest, but in everything else as well: non-drinker, non-smoker, big-time factotum with the Dominicans on Pope's Quay – with the reverence the womenfolk especially had for the white-robed Order of Preachers, a feat of real one-upmanship. Maybe it was this, maybe some genuinely nascent sense of upward mobility, but Jimmy did carry about with him an unmistakable aura of respectability. He was always well-dressed; he favoured sable or dark suits, white shirts, and a smart 'couteau' hat. In this, he stood out from the other menfolk in our life, as he did in manner and demeanour too: for he was modest, diffident, full of old-world courtesies like shaking hands with people when he met them or holding the door open to let them in. His sights were clearly set on his brand of middle-class morality, and his clear ambition was to be taken for a fully paid up member of the middle class. Though by rank and station he was not yet one, in the meantime he did all he could to reach that enviable state. If good nature and good breeding were to be the criteria, Uncle Jimmy had long since made the grade.

He had a hard old life of it. His first job was with Ryan's Soap and Candle Works on Pope's Quay, a job which ended with the gaffer noting that he was constantly coughing in the melting tallow-fumes, a sign of worse to come. So he is given his cards and a week's wages and told to lie up for a bit till he's better, but not to bother coming back because his job is gone. So for most of the forty-odd years that follow, he is a navvy, a road-maker, a dock-worker, all death and destruction to his ailing lungs; but he survives them and outlives all his Ryan's workmates to become in time the heart and centre of our whole singing tribe.

I came on him once while he was working in a gang laying tar on the roadway in Blarney Street. There he was belting out the molten tar from the buckets and then down on his knees rolling it with a flat-iron, the fumes rising up in his face fit to kill. When that job ran out, I saw him later loading hundredweight flour-sacks in a granary on the docks, the air thick with the white powder-fog, another surefire killer. Neither had the slightest effect on his singing, which got better and stronger the more fumes and vapours he took in.

So the years went by and everyone got to know him.

Births, deaths and marriages, games, victory-parades, parties for going away and parties for coming home – he was asked to them all, he always came, and he was often the only sober man in the place. Blessed he was by some uncanny ability to rise wave by wave with the drink-levels and sooner or later out-top them all. In those years, he would come over to our house and sing in harmony with us the songs we were learning at school, sometimes his lovely mellow tenor turning my reedy soprano into pure melted gold. This would be in something like the Brahms Lullaby in Irish, neither one nor other of us having the least idea what the words meant; but that didn't matter, the sound was all.

> Soondereeha iss law, iss na hangill i draw,
> Sondereeha is law, is na hah-in-gill i draw.

(What we were singing were the words – *Suaimhneas oíche is lá, is na haingil i dtráth* – 'Tranquil night-time and noon, with the angels in tune.')

What stood to Jimmy mightily in those days was the choir of the revered Dominicans, a polished and perfectionist outfit if ever there was one. That wasn't at all exceptional, for it was a time for songs and singing of which 'sweet singing in the choir' was a part. Home, choir, pub, all became one in a single golden alchemy of sound.

So, when Jimmy Doyle up the road shot the high wire at Mass on Sunday morning with his searing tenor 'Jey-ey-rus-al-em', the other male voices who had sung note for note with him in 'The Mountain' the night before would intercept his rocket in mid-flight and bring him safely down in close bass-baritone formation. Incidentally, the 'Mountain' version was the secular 'Jerusalem' sung by the American tenor Richard Crooks, who sang from a wheelchair, driving half the tenors of Cork out of their minds trying to get into one to be as good as him. Father Mac, the choirmaster, a decent man and fond of a jar himself, had the good sense to know that 'The Mountain' was a better training-ground than any choir-loft for his bevy of troubadors. So he turned the blind eye – and deaf ear – on them as he passed by on Saturday nights, hearing his 'larks in the clear air' singing their hearts out in notes that he hoped wouldn't be choked by fog and smoke and hangovers when they got to his loft the following morning.

He wasn't the only choir-master around, nor was he the best. That was surely Aloys Fleischmann, a Bavarian who came originally as a refugee from Germany and stayed on to make the rough-and-ready boys of Shandon Street and Blackpool into a Vienna Boys Choir of his very own. Gerard Brady of the Dominicans – Uncle Jimmy's choir – was aloof and exacting and always worked to the strengths of his men and women, never letting them take on anything new which, on big festive occasions, could easily go off the rails. And in tow with him, his second-string conductor, was Harry Whitehouse, a benign white-whale of a man with a bad stammer – until he sang, when what came out was such a golden glory that you'd wonder to God why the perfectionist Gerard Brady bothered with a choir at all and didn't let Harry do the singing himself.

Our Uncle Jimmy had absorbed all this over the years and would bring it out in time. He had a way of phrasing the words of a song, songs we all knew, which gave them a new meaning and made them sound as if you were hearing them for the first time. His 'Oft in the Stilly Night', with our sister Lil in harmony, was a sure way of restoring the peace on one of those stormy Christmas nights. But then there was his other side, taken from his lifelong sobriety or maybe inbred from his tungsten mother, 'Nanny Apples'; for he was also the only one who could shake us out of the Jesus-weeps, with which the family was cursed whenever a tearjerker session came on.

Father, for instance, battle-scarred soldier though he was, could never get through the ballad about the 1798 Wicklow freedom-fighter 'Michael Dwyer' without weeping. When the big crying-verse came on, the one in which 'up stood the brave MacAllister, the weak and wounded man' to give his life to save his trapped comrades, he'd start to blubber and the whole house would be in a black knot trying to get him through; which of course would only make him twice as bad, twice as determined to carry on. That could have been the sad end of many a singing night but for Jimmy with one of his rabble-rousing choruses, 'The Bould Thady Quill', a full-throated ballad about Cork's holy trinity of hurling, drinking and politics, or Percy French's 'Phil the Fluter's Ball' or 'Tread on the Tail of Me Coat.' In the course of that, he'd stand out in the middle of the floor and throw off his coat to challenge us all:

> I cleaned up the Finnegan faction
> And licked all the Murphys afloat;
> If you're in for a row or a ruction,
> Just tread on the tail of me coat.

As the years passed, he learned new songs. He seemed to put more meaning into them, as his paced and plangent voice caressed the words, telling you with every line that he knew what they meant, though he would never do anything so foolish as to break up and weep about it. The only time we ever saw him give in to anything like that was the morning he came to tell us that his mother, our 'Nanny Apples', had died. Like a circus comic he looked then, with the tears running down his lined and craggy face and falling like raindrops from the point of his chin. Later, when his wife died, leaving him with five young children to look after, he didn't have time for crying or for anything much else either, though you would sometimes hear the gulp in his throat when he got to singing 'Absence':

Oftimes between long shadows on the grass
One little ray of sunlight seems to pass;
My eyes grow dim with tenderness the while,
Thinking I see thee, thinking I see thee smile.

But he'd get through somehow. The family was reared, the four lovely girls were married and his only son had become a priest. He should have been old by then but he was never old; right up to the end he had the long swinging stride of an agile man, always active, always busy about some new and urgent work. So we brought him everywhere with us: to all the weddings and christenings, to the hurling and football matches, and a whole new generation of songsters grew up around him and got to know when he was there.

Man alive, what torrents and rivers of sound we made together then, as we swung with him on the high lines of 'Let Me Like a Soldier Fall' or with 'way down upon the Swanee River.' A one-stop, one-shop Mormon Tabernacle Choir we were together then, pilgrims caught up in a swelling chorus of joy, unpurchasable to any but those who were poor enough to have nothing else but that in the world.

As he got older, Jimmy learnt new songs and sang them better, with more punch and vigour, than any of us younger ones around him: like the Beach Boys, 'Sloop John B.' which he turned into one of our new anthems at the drinking-and-

singing sessions after the big hurling games, with a new generation of throatful choristers joining in, none of them seeing
the living irony in the old man's words:

We sailed on the Sloop John B.,
My grandpappy and me,
All over the seven seas we did roam.
Went drinking all night,
Got into a fight,
I feel so broke-up I wanna go home.

Years later, when he came to visit me in Dublin, I would
go off to work in the mornings, leaving him at the record-
player with a pile of discs beside him. When I came back
hours later, there he'd be, listening intently to the same
music over and over: Mozart, Beethoven, Brahms, as well as
the more popular Puccini, Verdi and Gilbert and Sullivan. It
was all familiar to him from long, happy nights in the 'gods'
of the Opera House long ago when one of the touring com-
panies came to Cork. And so it remained right down to the
end, music, songs, all and every kind and variety of them,
that and agonies and ecstasies of Cork hurling – those would
make a full and self-sufficient life for him down to the finishing line.

As luck would have it, his last outing brought both these
strands together. It was a wedding, that of one of his grand-
nephews, our big brother Ken's son, Tim Murphy, then captain of the Cork senior hurling team. It would be over 60
years since our Uncle Jimmy had pulled on a jersey himself;
there's a photograph of him from that time in which the little mascot out front is that eldest brother of ours, then a boy
of three. He was, as always, unsuppressible: old songs for
the old, young songs for the young – but young and old
came together in a last hurrah for what had by then become

his signature tune, a song on which, for us, he has put his stamp and mark forever:

> Those were the days, my friends,
> We thought they'd never end,
> We'd sing and dance forever and a day;
> We'd live the life we choose,
> We'd fight and never lose,
> Those were the days, my friends, those were the days.

I write it here, not in nostalgia nor in the pain of reminiscence, but in jubilation for someone who sang for love and whose ha'p'orth of songs made us celebrate with him through short but not inglorious years.

10

A Bicycle in the Hallway

THE Great War took a deadly number of Irish lives; some 50,000 in all; the Dublins, the Munsters, the Connaught Rangers and the Ulster and Leinster Rifles all contributed their share. But once, in the course of it, something happened which, in the microcosm of our private little world, was to have an even more profound and far-reaching effect. Our father was hit with shell-shrapnel in the head and chest, which got him out of the front line and eventually home for a brief period of leave, a leave which, nine months later, would produce his first son, named after him, our eldest brother, Kennedy.

That month of May 1916 when he was born was a troubled time in the life of Ireland. Not alone was the war taking its deadly toll but, what would become more crucial to the story of Ireland ... a few weeks before Kennedy's arrival ... the Easter Rising had taken place. Compared to the slaughter in Flanders, it was a storm in a teacup. Father would say: 'I often saw more shootin' done before me breakfast!' But it was a seminal event which awakened the spirit of Irish separatism, leading six short years later to the setting up of the Irish Free State and a large measure of national independence. So, when Father returned to 'a fit country for heroes to live in', in Ireland's case the heroes were no longer those of the Somme, Ypres and the Marne, but the freedom-fighters of 1916 and their successors: the Irish Republican Army of Michael Collins, Seán Tracey and Dan Breen; and Cork's own Tom Barry, who had himself been in the British Army throughout the war and now put his military skills and training to effect as the guerrilla strategist of the West Cork Flying Column.

For our father, the 'fit country for heroes' meant the fourth-floor tenement rooms on Blarney Street, the night-shift on the railway in Kilbarry, and the brief amnesiac of Curry's pub on a Saturday night when they could sing to their hearts' content the old tunes of glory – so different from Siegfried Sassoon's 'scarlet Majors at the Base, who sped glum heroes up the line to death' – while they sat 'guzzling and gulping in the best hotel'.

That infant son of his would see much death and destruction about him in his fourth-floor eyrie. The great flu epidemic of 1919 swept away a sister and a pair of twins – one of them named, like me, after Grandfather 'William'. A few years later and another three were gone, all victims of rampant disease and malnutrition.

So it is no exaggeration to say that, for this boy, survival was the main aim: just to grow up to be a man, nothing more, and maybe enjoy a few years of such fun-and-games as were to be had, with nothing higher or more lofty for ideals and ambitions.

How, where and why did he develop perspectives

beyond that? The upward thrust of the time was indeed part of it – that tenth-world country which had been raped of its resources for centuries, with no outlets for its coolie sons but what they might find at the far side of the Atlantic, if ever they could get there. Now, they were suddenly free to find and develop outlets at home. There were vague whisperings from far-off places, like the new Irish civil service then opening up; and new words like 'education' and 'scholarships' which would crop up every now and then. But the prevailing view was that a boy was wasting his time on such frills and flounces when he could be 'out earning'.

The Christian Brothers were indeed the major influence, with their schools in all the poor places and their pupils the ragamuffin riff-raff of the streets and back-lanes. In my own time, it was nothing unusual to see half a dozen of them come to school barefoot. School being compulsory up to the age of fourteen, they had to be there; otherwise they would not have come. Once they became fourteen, there was but one aim – to get up and get out; anything at all would do, any job once it helped to keep the home fires burning. Messenger-boys proliferated, pedalling furiously up and down the steep hills of Cork on heavily-laden panier-bikes, with the silver lining of a ten-bob note beckoning every Saturday night, but also with a death-sentence hanging over them when they got to eighteen, the age at which they had to be paid men's wages; then they were out. That was the end of many a young man's dream. The *Innisfallen* was the next stop, thence to the lump-contractors of London, Birmingham and Coventry. And the annual Christmas visit home to show they were still alive.

Wherever it came from, whatever the drive, blind trust or inspired hoping, this terminal life was not to be for any of us. Others followed their fathers into small jobs on the buses or railway, but Father would swear he would rather be dead than see any of us with the 'badge of servitude' – the thick black corduroys which was the standard uniform for the rail-waymen of his time.

When, later, my third brother John did briefly get a job as a railway porter and worked beside him, Father deeply resented it. And, when at weekends, with the slim riches of his porterage to hand, the young man could afford to dress up in style, making him look quite the gentleman, Father could never seem to forget the black corduroy under the fine crombie, and could not conceal his delight when finally he left to take up a job as a junior clerk with a miserly Scrooge who paid him half the money but who took him out of his caterpillar bondage. It all goes to show that riches maketh not the man, nor that by bread alone doth man live, but by every dream that keeps his self-respect alive.

Later again, our brother Jim got to be a bus-conductor, a clean and a well-paid job; but it too was marked with the bondage sign. Father was dead by then but, even if he were around, he might not have fought too hard against it. For this 'wild colonial boy' had broken ranks before and could be relied on to do so again and again. He had left school because of a teacher he hated, then ran away from home to join the army – all of which carried echoes of Father's own progress some forty years earlier, when he swapped the odours of the back-lanes of Cork for the sunny climes of Africa and the bear's hug of the doughty Boers. In this sturdy, loveable but unruly boy, he must surely have seen the mirror image of himself, a fiery particle with ungovernable strengths, one of which was a good mind, but an even better and stronger will to go with it, a hazardous mixture which in time would lead to some alarming combustions.

Robbing orchards, getting into fights with anyone who

showed the least sign of wanting to fight with him, being hauled home by the police and threatened with detention in Greenmount, the local Reformatory School – a regular heartscald of a boy he was, our Jim, the most heart-scalding part of him being that he was the cleverest and most inventive of us all. Yet neither Father nor Mother could ever find it in them to say a cross word to him. He was the black sheep, the prodigal son wasting his time and energies wherever he went – and then ending up with the fatted calf laid out for him in joyous celebration of his merely continuing to be alive.

All this was in stark contrast to our eldest brother Kennedy, who, whatever instinct was in him or whatever influences were working on him, had his sights set on the right targets from the start.

I was all of five when we bade a farewell to our tenement rooms, yet I have a clear memory of him sitting to one side at a small table with the hiss of the paraffin-lamp on the mantelshelf above him and the coals burning red through the three-barred grate below. He must have been looking at something – I know now it had to be books – but books mean little to a child of five. What I see is the bent head, the darkness coming in through the windows, with the bells of Shandon ringing out the quarter-hours from up the street. That, and the web of silence Mother seems to weave about him – the illiterate who at the age of eight had her head bent above the broom on a flax-mill floor and was seeing to it now that nothing like that would ever happen to any of us.

For we are in this new Ireland now, with the dawn of freedom lighting up the horizon. True, the memory of wars and pensions and separation-money is still there; like the enslaved children of Israel fattening off the fleshpots of

Egypt, 'We were better off under the British' they would sometimes say. But those brightening horizons were there, the promised lands were no longer mere pie-in-the-sky for a people who but a short time before could do no more than pray that their future might bring better than their past. If it did, they were lucky. If it did not, so be it. For now, they had enough to eat, there was a roof over their heads, and '*is giorra cabhair Dé ná an doras*' – God's help was nearer than the door.

That is the time and this the atmosphere in which big brother Ken is growing up. The wind of change is blowing, fanned by the spartan Christian Brothers, which in time will make a new time for us all. The boy born a few weeks after the Easter Rising will hear and take in the ideas of that time, chief of which is the new-made nation-in-the-making in which, with work and effort, he may one day take part.

Across the road from us, in what looked like a long dark hallway full of shelves of fabrics and cloths and woollen goods is Lorton's Clothes Shop. It is warm and feather-dry like the inside of a nest, with rich and purring scents coming off the new-made cloth; an Aladdin's Cave where we sometimes go with our mother when she has a few shillings to spend. The lady of the house, Mrs Lorton, is a great spreading chestnut-tree of a woman with a large family of her own. Maybe that's what she and Mother have in common, because surely they have nothing else. With the shelves piled high with things we could never buy, and with the till constantly ringing its merry tune, there's no fear that we will ever have anything like the Lortons, a rich man's home, with velvets and velours, silks and satins to cushion and featherbed their way.

But they have this one boy who is unlike the rest of them; he is thin and weak, he is always coughing and fighting for breath. In some ways, our sister Eily would have been the mirror image of him but for the fact that he is well-protected and well-nurtured, while she has nothing but the love in a cold climate we can give. But both were cherished for what they were and both manage miraculously to be always in great good spirits. In some ways, they were to be the heart and centre of their homes.

This boy's name is Paddy and he and Ken become friends. Paddy is in and out of our place all the time; he doesn't seem to mind the four flights up, the cats, the smells, the prowling eyes of Mad Annie, nor Miss Goggin whispering the Rosary like a ghost in the dark at all hours.

Mr Lorton is a big stony man and is something very important in the world. His name sometimes appears in the *Echo*, 'Andrew Lorton P.C.', with a photograph showing a face hewn from granite. But big and important as he is, he will always break into a smile whenever he sees one of us – which isn't too often, since we have no good reason to be in the great man's presence.

I suspect now that the reason he smiles at us was that he likes big brother Ken – and likes him more especially for the friendship that has grown up between him and his ailing son. The fact that so fine and healthy a boy – by common consent, a clever boy too – could be his son Paddy's best friend surely means that there can be nothing much wrong with *him*.

Paddy is the youngest of the family; there's a whole squad of brothers and sisters before him. All those older ones had grown up in the heyday of the British Empire, of which Ireland, a fevered and dejected limb, was then a part. So the fruits of Empire were there for them to take, those of them strong and brave enough to take them. Such a one was the oldest brother, who had fixed his sights on the rich and exotic British Colonial Service – in India, South Africa, Canada, any of the dominions of 'our far-flung battle-line'. And that's where he goes, away off to a life of service to King and Country in the Indian Civil Service. The name and fame of his achievement stays around long after him, so much so that he is the high-flyer for all others to follow when their time comes. It was through this eldest Lorton boy that the words 'civil service' first come to be spoken in our house.

For up to that, if it was class-distinction we were looking for, we need to look no farther than our cousin Mick McGrath, a petty-officer in the British Navy; or a neighbour Jack Healy, who did a policy-round for the Royal Liver; or, holy of holies, a job in a pawnbroker's, of which, alas, there were plenty – and we were familiar with not a few.

But a job in the civil service was away beyond all that. Up in the stars it was, where only the very clever and the very best could hope to be! For the lucky one, at one mighty bound he was out of the pit of the working or unemployed class; he had a white-collar job with his pay and pension guaranteed, a long way up the dizzy climb to class-distinction. But India was a long way off and strange things could happen there: riots and revolutions, floods and famines and disasters of all kinds – let alone women with dark skins and red weals on their foreheads. Glory be to God, what would become of our family pride if the boy came home with a nightmare like that!

But now these new sounds begin to be heard, these new lights begin to appear on the horizon. Dickie Shortland lived up the road from us: a cherub with burning blue eyes which burnt, some said, because he had such brains behind them; he goes in for this civil service – wonder of wonders, it's the home-grown Irish one. More wonderful still, he gets it. He's the first of his kind and will be the pathfinder for a whole new generation.

When the news gets round, his mother is queen-of-the-May. She now is a cut above buttermilk! All the other mothers round about look up to her. From then on, the books and the paraffin-lamps hissing on the mantelshelf begin to have new significance.

When night comes down, there's this whistling from the street below and Mother goes to the big front window, the rusted pulleys and rotten ropes screeching in agony as she pulls it up.

'Mrs Murphy, will Kennedy be out?' comes the cry from down below.

'He's not, he's studying.'

(To one side and drowsed with the heat from the fire, I'm thinking: so that's what he's doing with those books – 'studying'.)

'He told us to call, he said he'd come out when he's finished. Tell him it's us.'

'Who's us?'

A babble of names comes out but at the end comes – 'Dickie Shortland ... Paddy Lorton ... Finbarr Lynch.'

'He'll be out in a minute so.'

Down comes the window, the studying will wait: Dickie Shortland, soon to be the civil service hero; Paddy Lorton, the boy with his brother in the Indian Civil Service; Finbarr Lynch from under Shandon, whose father is a tailor in a grand shop on Patrick Street – another job where you didn't have to take off your coat to work; that's enough to ring the jackpot on Mother's approval: in that company Ken is already on his way to white-collar ascendancy! (Note in passing: Finbarr Lynch's brothers were big hurling names with the Glen Rovers; forty years on, one of them, Jack, will become Taoiseach.)

It is all part of the rituals and dance of a newly emergent nation: people liberated so that they have hope, though some still have a backward glance to the *ancien régime*. Paddy Lorton, with chronic asthma challenging his every breath – the word was hardly known in those years – goes off to South Africa where it is said the dry air on the plateau above Cape Town will be good for his ailing lungs. We never hear of him again. But that brother of his, and Dickie Shortland later, have beckoned us to civil servitude, a magic wand that soon will touch us all. Finbarr and Jack Lynch will both end up there; others who come along later will strive for white-collar fame and fortune too. In all this, the Christian Brothers are father and mother to us, teacher and tyrant too. It is indeed a rising tide – though for us in our two-pair back at Goulnaspurra it is yet but the waters lapping at our feet.

For I am five and I am standing at the window watching the world go by. Suddenly looking down on the Green Garden, I see what looks like a full packet of Half-Time-Jimmy lying on the grass.

Now you want to know what a Half-Time-Jimmy is. It's a chocolate bar in squares, twelve of them, with nuts and currants all through. It is the best, most luscious chocolate in the world. Even if I don't know it's the best, the price should tell me: it's sixpence – a 'tanner' we call it – more money than I have ever seen. There's this picture of a soccer-field on the wrapper, with a player shooting at goal, and the crowd behind him cheering. And I'm there in the middle, I am Half-Time-Jimmy. The excitement is mighty and I would love it to stay like that: just stand there and be the hero for all the crowd to cheer. But the chocolate wins out and I tear open the wrapper and get at the chocolate inside. Half-Time-Jimmy is gone now and I'll never have another sixpence again.

But this time it's free: if it is one. I look again and it is still there. The light is going; it's getting dark, maybe it's playing tricks on me? I make my way down the dark stairs, with Miss Goggin's cats getting ready for their nightly prowl and Mad Annie peering with her wild eyes to drag me in. But I get safely by and then I'm out on Blarney Street, with only the bars of the Green Garden before me.

Once through them and I'm there, I have the Half-Time-Jimmy; it's all mine. But first I must test the bars to make sure my head will fit through. If I don't do that and my head gets stuck, the Guards will have to be called to drive wedge-blocks in above and below me to set me free. But I am five; I have only a little button of a head and no bars will stop me getting at my Half-Time-Jimmy. Is it real? Can I possibly have such luck? I go through and lift it. It is a full brand-new Half-Time-Jimmy all for myself alone!

I never stop to think that maybe someone has poisoned it and the *Echo* will have the story tomorrow – 'Boy dies from chocolate poisoning' – like my pal Pa Mac when the wall fell on him right beside the Green Garden and killed him. But that can wait. All I know is that this is a full Half-Time-Jimmy and it's mine and I am going to eat it before whatever fool lost it or left it comes back to take it away.

Twelve squares of chocolate may seem a lot. You'd think you might be able to stretch it out a bit, maybe even keep some for later? But I have it, it's a gift from God – or some poor eejit who lost or mislaid it – so it had better be gone before God or the eejit comes back. I sit there and eat, square by square, while the Shandon bells ring out the quarter-hours and play those lovely airs: 'The Minstrel Boy', 'Believe Me If All Those Endearing Young Charms', 'The Blue Bells of Scotland'. And the drop-and-lift of the sound rising and falling over the roofs and gables mixed with the taste and savour of the Half-Time-Jimmy runs into the roots of my soul. I am there a long time hidden under the stairs where no one will see me. But at last it is gone and I come out.

It is pitch-dark on the stairs now and the four flights up are a nightmare. The Half-Time-Jimmy hero of a while back is no hero at all now, but face them he must. A cat howls and Annie Downey's door creaks. There is the mad woman inside, her hair down on her face and she has a red-hot poker in her hand. Half-Time-Jimmy shrieks in terror and his mother shrieks in answer from the floor above.

'Where were ye, ye caffler? They're all out lookin' for ye; you'll be the death of me!'

So I am safe, she is there, the dim light from the paraffin-lamp lights up the landing above me. But on that landing I see a sight that will never leave me. It is a brand new bicycle, its spokes gleaming in the lamplit gloom and its black enamel chain-case smooth as water on a moonlit night.

'It's Ken's,' Mother tells me. 'It's for his new job in the civil service.'

Gradually, it sinks in: he has got this civil service exam and job; but the job will be in Limerick and, to save the train-fare at weekends, this new bicycle will bring him home.

Limerick, civil service, weekend – the words mean little to Half-Time-Jimmy. He goes back out onto the dark landing, now a magic and enchanted place with this wonderful new bicycle to prove it. Maybe, with luck, one day he can have a thing like that too!

11

Heroes and Heroines

With all this talk of soldiers and soldiering about me, you might think the killer instinct was something I should have been born with, but it was not. In this, maybe I am a bit like many Irishmen, big on 'howlin' and fightin' but small on it when real trouble looms. Father's permanent mood was one of nostalgia for his fighting days, mixed with occasional bouts of the most alarming tearfulness. True, he could burst into a rage when something got to him – like that night in Curry's when someone called one-legged Uncle Johnny a 'fuckin' cripple', and Father hit him so hard that he drove his head through the window. Another time our cousin 'Legsy' Sullivan, who was a sergeant with the Munsters – and for good measure, middleweight champion of the British Army – stood out in full uniform in the middle of the road as the Black-and-Tans came up Shandon Street in Crossley tenders waving their revolvers and addressed them in these comradely terms: 'Get down out of that, ye scum of English scuts. We fought for ye on the Somme and the Marne and in Flanders and now, bejasus, here ye are with yeer tanks and yeer guns frightenin' the life out of innocent people. Get down outa that, if there's a man among ye, and I'll fight the whole fuckin' lot of ye single-handed.'

True or false, it makes a stirring story. And there were others. First cousin Jackie Buckley, Phil's brother, was also a British Army boxing champion. There was a photograph of him on the wall at home, as revered as the pictures of Our Lady and the Sacred Heart. It showed a crouched and feline figure with a ferocious scowl squaring up to some adversary, head down and gloved fists at the ready. No one noticed the nice lighting and the studio backdrop; it's all a fake – but he's our cousin and our hero; back off all challenges to our name and fame! Before ever he got to the Army, Jackie had done his boxing with 'Sunnyside' off Blarney Street, the North Side club, and later, when he went to England with his mother Aggie Munn, with a club near the docks at Wapping.

He was of the same stuff as 'Legsy', the kind that made the world-title names of the Irish-Americans, John L. Sullivan, Jimmy Braddock, 'Gentleman' Jim Corbett. A dynasty of prize-fighters the Irish in America were then, 'white niggers' who held the world title unchallenged until a new breed of black ones came along.

What's more, we had our own local home-grown champion, Jack Doyle from The Holy Ground in the Cove of Cork, who, again after a spell with the British Army, went on to be a contender for the heavyweight world title.

Tall, dark and handsome, with a mane of jet-black hair, Doyle was the 'Gorgeous Gael'. Whenever he was in a fight, the city stopped, with news flashes coming up hourly on a pre-historic neon-printer on Patrick Street and special Stop Press editions of the *Echo* and the *Examiner*. Stories went the rounds of millionaire Jack handing out five-pound notes to his friends to light their cigars with and gallons of champagne being quaffed to celebrate his victories. Meanwhile up and down the narrow streets we went, roaring defiance in each other's ears:

I am Jack Doyle from Erin's Isle,
Lie down, ye hoor, lie down

never for an instant thinking that that might have a more sinister meaning than lying down in the ring.

Jack's prowess came to an end one night when he was knocked out in the first round by an ancient English pug, Eddie Phillips. Some said that Jack was drunk, others that Phillips had hit him below the belt, others still that an enemy had put grease on the canvas and Jack had slipped. Whatever the cause, he was out for the count. And all his fanatic hero-worshippers were out along with him.

He did make a come-back, but not as a boxer. For the fact is that the 'Gorgeous Gael' could sing – after the Phillips débâcle, some said an awful lot better than he could fight. He had married Movita, a petite Hollywood starlet, and Cork went wild with delight when they came to sing for us. Hordes of star-struck and love-crazed girls screamed in ecstasy as the chrome-plated Chrysler drew up at the Savoy and the Gorgeous One got out with the petite Movita beside him.

It was – 'Come back Jack' then, 'all is forgiven'. I am all of twelve by now, but some small sceptic voice speaks up inside me: there are no heroes, it says, only dead ones; and Jack Doyle died the night Eddie Phillips knocked him out of the ring.

The couple sang and charmed us and we took them to our hearts. But, any more than the boxing, it was not to last. The story goes that one night when Movita was being fêted

by the Cork grandees, she came back to the Victoria Hotel
where they were staying to find Jack stoned out of his mind,
but still ca-pable of the bitter word. He asked her about the
party and how she had got on.

'I suppose they were all killed admiring you?'

'Indeed, they were,' she said. 'They were very nice to me
indeed.'

'And what did they find to admire about you?'

'Well,' she gallantly recalled, 'some admired my face,
some my hair, some my hands, some my legs.'

'Did any of them admire your bum?'

'No, darling,' la petite Mexicaine replied. 'None of them
mentioned you.'

There must have been a good side to poor Jack, though.
When he was at the height of his fame and the big money
was rolling in, he gave his mother the present of a fine
house in London. And when the bad times came, taking
defeat with the same stoic swagger as he had once taken
victory, he would never countenance the idea that she
might sell it to help him. He lived on to a ripe old age, the
last years of which were spent in a London boarding-house,
still managing to make some sort of a living from his gigs
in any of the Irish pubs that would have him.

Yes, he told an RTE interviewer one night when he was
drawing near the end of his days, he had seen the good times
when he was on top of the world; he would take the bad
times in the same spirit. Maybe he was a bigger hero than we
thought. And maybe the down-and-out was a better man
than the 'Gorgeous Gael' had ever been.

They were the Olympian heights; we were on the foothills
below. Soccer, hurling, football – anything at all would do to

earn a moment of glory, the hero-worshipped crown. For a time I cherished an unholy ambition to die on the field, so becoming the ultimate object of hero-worship, a martyr for the cause. There were a few occasions when I got close to it. Once when we put together enough penny 'scrips' to buy a real football, our road took on the next road in a cup match. The cup was a pearl of great price, handmade from the silver-paper in cigarette packets picked up along the street! This sterling trophy would be carried head-high up and down the road after our great victory. And all the neighbours would be at their doors cheering us. A bloody and bandaged hero would be best of all with echoes of – 'home they brought their warrior dead'! On the day in question, I play a blinder. I'm everywhere, back with the backs when needed, up with the forwards when a score is on. But suddenly I'm on the flat of my back, levelled, wounded. I'm twelve but my heart has given out. Unless the hero can be got back into play, all is lost. It is my moment of greatness. I am the focus of all eyes.

My greatness is short-lived. Tommy Neenan, a blonde little weasel, is our team-captain. 'Get up outa that for Jasus sake and stop coddin'! Five minutes more and you can die all you fuckin' like.' A boot in the backside has me on my feet and the game goes on. Heroes deserve better. It is the last time I will be a martyr for the cause.

The second event brings even less glory. Heroes that we are, an expected feature of our game is that we be able to fight as well as win. A team-mate who cannot fight is a passenger to be left where he should be, on the sideline. 'We'll beat ye first and fight ye after' is a common opening.

My time comes at last: I'm fouled, I hit out. The next thing I'm into it. A ring is formed with two Battling Sikis pummelling the devil out of each other. There's cheers and shouts and blood-curdling exhortations: 'Give him the cow's dig!' 'Give him the rabbit punch!' I feel nothing, though I must be getting hit; then my fist collides with something – a lump of dried dough, but when I look it's my antagonist's face and there's blood all over it.

Suddenly there's this whimpering sound and someone is running away. It's him. I run after him trying to catch up, with the whole crowd following. The match is abandoned, Tommy Neenan and Co. have me up on their shoulders: I am a hero at last. And off down the road we go, roaring our victory anthem:

We are the Rovers, what cannot be knocked out,
In hurling, in football, in anything at all ...

But something inside me is dark and bleak and unhappy. All I want to do is get down and go home and wash the blood off my face and hands. But before that I want to do something else. I want to go after and catch up with the little chap whose bloody nose is all over me and tell him I'm sorry. I suppose I'll never make a hero now.

Real heroes are made of sterner stuff. Tarzan swinging out of the eucalyptus trees on the Amazon to rescue Jane and Boy from the murderous rubber-planters – that's a hero for you! When it turns out that in real life he is Johnny Weissmuller, freestyle champion of the world, we're all down to the Eglington Street baths flailing the life out of ourselves with the crawl-kick and gulping chlorinated water by the gallon.

Buck Jones, Hopalong Cassidy, Roy Rogers on snow-white 'Trigger' – those are heroes too. We're each and every one of them when our local cinema, The Hall, disgorges its nightful of cowboys and we go roaring down Shandon Street, belting the hell out of our backsides to get Trigger ahead of the Red Indians. Oh, bliss it is to be a hero then, with a hundred and one other heroes galloping along beside you.

And then there were the living heroes, the ones we could see. Hurling is our great game and Cork one of its heartlands. For several years, Jack Lynch played with the Glen Rovers and Cork All-Ireland teams. One night after they had won the All-Ireland, the team came into Glanmire Station and, out there in front on the open-topped bus he was, our very own home-grown hero, from under Shandon Steeple up the road, with the crowds of Cork to celebrate him. 'One hour of glorious life is worth an age without a name'; if there was an air to it, we'd sing it. Nor was he the greatest.

That was surely Christy Ring, small and slight, a blonde cherub with forget-me-not eyes, up from the village of Cloyne in south Cork when we first saw him, and out to play for our northside 'Glen'. Hurlers in Cork are like matadors in Madrid; like them, in a few years his cherub face will be marked and lined with the scars of many an encounter. That was the stuff of hero-worship, of the songs and ballads written about him:

> Come gather round me boys tonight and raise your glasses
>> high,
> Come Rockies, Barrs and Rovers stars, let welcome hit the sky;
> Let bonfires blaze in heroes' praise, let Shandon's belfry
>> ring,
> For homeward bound with hurling crown comes gallant
>> Christy Ring.

> When we were young we read in school in the days of old
> How young Setanta showed his worth with shield and spear of
>> gold,
> As hurling hard on royal sward he'd hurling heroes fling;
> My soul, today, he'd yield the sway if he met Christy Ring.

Bryan MacMahon's ballad catches the idiom: gladiator in the dust, Ben Hur in the chariot-race, bullfighter in the blood-and-sand, prizefighter in the ring, the brave exhausted huskie following 'the call of the wild' in Jack London – all of them would have loved the blood and bones of Cork-born Christy Ring.

Yes, there was a madness there to be sure, but a madness touched with something else: the exaltation of the fight to a finish, a fight tempered by great skills greatly applied: the ball hopping like a hobgoblin on his hurley, speed, strength, fire bursting from the small blonde fireball weaving and streaking in the tumult of the goalmouth; and, with but a hairsbreadth of space, the strike at goal, so straight and deadly that nothing could stop it. And it went on for years, feats of strength and solo-runs that will be printed forever on our minds.

Years later, when his hurling days are done, I invite him to join me on one of my Eve-of-All-Ireland television talk-shows. He says 'No' – talk is not his game.

He would have nothing to say that hadn't been said earlier and better by people whose game it was. All he knows about is hurling and what he has to say about that was said long ago on the playing field in the only way he knew. He reminds me then of that shy young matador in Hemingway's *The Sun Also Rises:* the bull's horn plunging at him and death in the afternoon – it is the only language he can speak. He has no other words, no other talents to offer the infatuated Lady Brett, who is fantasising him into her version of the poet-hero. But there is no poetry there, just that sole primary skill; that, and an innocence beyond words. Yet therein is a greatness which only the God who makes great bullfighters – and great hurlers – will understand.

I leave the last word on Christy Ring with Uncle Jimmy's

son, first cousin John Buckley, a missionary priest in Africa. He is coming out after saying Mass on a September Sunday morning. Suddenly, whatever trick the light is playing on him, he sees in the grass about him the green sward of Dublin's Croke Park on a September Sunday, All-Ireland Hurling day. And it all comes back, the thrill of being a young hero-worshipper following his hero:

(NOTE: red and white are the Cork colours, black and amber the colours of arch-rivals Kilkenny.)

I remember well!
A child perched upon the rock that was my father's shoulders,
With wide innocent eyes taking in the waves of red and white,
Of black and amber,
And the green field lit by the bright sun.
Behind him the Lee mingled with the salt water,
And lovers walking the Marina heard the thunderous roar of
       rival crowds.

The year? 'Twas one near the mid-Forties,
The child, oblivious of a world scourged by Swastikas,
Names then unfamiliar surround him: Lynch, Langton, Maher
       – and young Ring.
Ring! Ring! Ring!

The child grew to manhood,
The father grew old to the echo of that sound.
Variations on a theme:
Ring, boy! Christy, boy! I wouldn't doubt ye, Ringey, boy!
Ring winning, Ring losing, Ring jubilant, Ring saddened
But always – Ring!

We were the faithful ones who first knelt in the dark silence of
       early Mass.
Under our arms, bread and butter wrapped in old newspapers,

Our precious tickets clutched in our trousers pockets,
And, after the 'Deo Gratias',
The anxious journey through the dreaded tunnel,
Past hay saved and not so saved,
To battlefields afar –
But always Ring!
He was our Cuchulain, the epitome of a glorious heritage!
Speed, skill, strength, courage, craft, composure –
All those gifts were his.

In vain did we in narrow streets, with broken sticks and paper
      ball,
Try to imitate him,
Only the dream remains.
Yet all those gifts were not his greatness,
Not for him the banality of studio lights,
Nor the profit of the quick sell;
Hurley in hand, boots in bag,
His was always the quiet exit.
His greatness was – he had the true perspective on all things.

And then there were the women. Heroics were not expected
of them, but they happened and in the most unlikely places
too. There was that Betsy with her mane of black hair tied up
in a bun and the face of an amazon, built for quarrel and conquest. She was from the Holy Ground in Cove, which may
have been holy once but for all our time was the favourite
haunt of soldiers and sailors from the forts and ships, a regular influx of likely lads intent upon one thing and that was
not the scenic beauty of Cork Harbour.

The 'Gorgeous Gael' Jack Doyle was from the Holy
Ground. Was that why they sang that charming little ditty –

    I am Jack Doyle from Erin's Isle,
    Lie down, ye hoor, lie down.

In proof of all this, on 15 August, Our Lady's Day, each year there would be this row at home about the same Holy Ground. Big sister Eily, despite the bad leg, could be a fetching little piece when she wanted to be and the annual Cove Regatta was a great event for such fetching little pieces to be. Father, being the old soldier that he was, knows well what the sideshows were in seaports such as Cove all over the world, so he will have none of it.

'Cove Regatta, my arse,' he will emphatically object; 'the girl will go to no such place.'

'But it's Our Lady's Day,' Mother will plead, taking the errant's part. There'll be a big parade and it'll be a great day out for her.'

'I know the "our ladies" that'll be on parade at the Cove Regatta,' he persists. 'No daughter of mine will be there.'

I wonder who the "our ladies" can be that he's talking about – until one such Cove Regatta day when he comes out with an even more colourful description: 'There'll be nothing down there but the usual – hoors and harlots and fellas coming after them with only the wan thing on their minds.'

To us, this of course makes it sound like a fascinating place – what with hoors and harlots and, better still, 'the wan thing'. That would make it a very special place indeed.

Being from the Holy Ground, there was nothing surer in that Betsy's life than that one day she would marry a sailor and, in due course, it being wartime, a sailor's widow when her man went down with His Majesty's *Dreadnought* in the Great War. Not, however, before leaving his calling-card in the form of six children, four sons and two daughters, all handsome as their sea-grieved mother and fanatically attached to her for the rest of her life. Her drowned Jack Tar had done her the signal service of leaving her with the full widow's pension. But, with six strapping youths to feed, that was a spit on a red-hot poker – so, she began to take in lodgers to help out. One of those in due course will be poor Tim Gahan, a big innocent slob of a man who, however, found the six noisy siblings no hindrance to a good night's sleep, especially when taken in the bed of their fecund mother. This in due time brought forth new fruits upon the bough, all blissfully unaware of the laws of wedlock, which they had a good right to be since they were born in wedlock in all but name.

For the specifics of that law were that, if Betsy once remarried, she would lose her pension, a wanton recklessness bringing no gain and much loss. So, she lived out her ife in what in those times would be regarded as mortal sin; a sin, though, which would surely be forgiven by a good God who would not blame a decent woman for tricking the civil law by staying married to a man who was dead and not getting married to one who was alive, both being an essential part of the wherewithal to keep the roof over their heads.

As for poor Tim Gahan, he was in no condition to object. God, Betsy, the children of both him and her dead Jack Tar – those were the pieces that held his world together. So, his goodly bedfellow could play ducks and drakes with the laws of God and man, the basic law of motherhood and provision being a far more urgent imperative. Through all those years, one way and another, the children of both her families were around her. The ones who went away regularly came home to visit and they would have these wild parties going far into the night, with great songs and carousing, and sometimes fistfights when one of them heard, or thought they heard, a slight upon their name and fame. But rows and ructions or peace and prosperity, there was our Betsy always in the midst of them, separating them, upbraiding them, cajoling them, by her will and

181

presence the 'mother of all of ye'.

In this she was both warrior and hero, telling us all in her rumbustious way that for a family to stay together the sun must never go down upon their anger. With her tigress instinct for that sole principle, this glorious, unkempt, disorderly bundle of energy always managed to draw her wayward and unruly flock back in line and lead them in the same direction: providing for them, chastising and cursing them, begging and coaxing them, but always there to be the heart and soul of them, never caring a jot or tittle what the rest of the world thought about the hardships and afflictions they brought on her. And in return she got the one thing she wanted: from boy and man, from girl and woman, from each and every one of them, she got their undying love. To us on the outside it didn't seem a lot; but to her inside her squalid and chaotic home, it made a safe haven for them all.

Then there was our Father's only sister, Aunt Nonie, the fattest woman in the world. The reason I can say this is that a little farther up Shandon Street was the second fattest woman in the world and she was a mere pimple compared to the great florid amplitude of my Aunt Nonie. The terrace of hovels on Drummy's Lawn where she lived must have been hundreds of years old; the roof-beams sagged, and the plaster inside and out was cracked and wrinkled like some seashell encrusted with age.

But, despite all that, it's a lovely warm place the way she has it. Over against the wall as you go in, there's this galleon of an oak-dresser, with saucers and plates slanting against the backboard, and cups, jugs, bowls and knick-knacks dangling from every inch of the wood. They must have been there since time began. She certainly could not afford them now. Her husband had died a long time ago. He was that Scot in a kilt, Hugh Miller, my grandfather William Murphy's great friend. Like battle-scarred Betsy's Jack Tar, he hadn't gone without leaving her with a squad of children for a keepsake; by the time they were looked after, there wasn't much left for buying knick-knacks for the dresser! But looked after they were and by her own labours too. Like our grandmother 'Nanny Apples', she was a fruit-dealer. Why fruit? With a toss of her cauliflower head and a laugh that was more a challenge than an answer, 'Is it fruit?' she'd say. 'Yerra boy, weren't we squezz out of fruit in the Garden of Eden the first day ever?'

She kept her stall at one side of the fountain where 'Nanny Apples' once used to be. The fountain was long disused and the wide dried-up basin made a fine prop for the trays of fruit, set up with showman cunning to catch the eye of the passers-by. From month to month, how the colours on those trays would change! In spring, the big yellow heads of the Jaffa oranges jostling against the pale green apples from South Africa; in July, with the heat, the velvet plums and amber gooseberries; in September, as the home-grown fruit came in, russets and pippins and rough brown pears, piled in mounds beside bananas blackening with ripeness, peaches blanched and powder-fine like ladies in retirement and grapes snug in their bed of cork – all finely arrayed about the great centrepiece of Aunt Nonie. When the big buying climax of Halloween approached, she would sit there with her hands folded under the shawl, the streetlights would come on and she would lift her eyes towards them: 'The light of heaven to us', she'd say. And the wrinkles would loosen on her face and her shadow would fall across the fruits as her hands went out over them, sorting them, touching them as she might have touched the skins of children, watching the trays empty and the stocks sell out – and money, money, thank God, thank God, and the end of another day!

No doubt there were comfortable people about, people 'assured of certain certainties', with good houses to go to and fat purses to keep them that way. Sometimes, if she had a slack hour, Aunt Nonie might dream about them, about a time when she could count on certainties too – when she'd buy a new shawl with tassels of thick wool, or a roll of new lino for the hovel floor, at the wild outside maybe rent a shop, a shining glittering glassy-palace of a place, with bottles of coloured sweets in the window and the smell of chocolate when you came in the door. But for her such dreams were a folly; they could never happen. Better take what you had and live without them.

Meanwhile, those others went by, 'her betters' she'd call them; they didn't have to know how the other half lived. But alone, savaged by life and derelict as she was, what she didn't know was that, even then, she had things she had neither the time nor the vanity to think she had, things that were far, far better.

For, with her man dead and her on her own, she was both hero and heroine at the same time, unbuffered by doles or the promise of pay, a prey if ever there was one to the slings and arrows of whatever outrageous fortune might befall. But it isn't the slave-striving nor the day-in-day-out fight for a living I now remember about her, but the toss of her great head in laughter and her raucous laugh flung in the teeth of a thousand woes. She would have had a good right to weep, like poor Job stuck on his dunghill – but one great shout from the core of her laughing heart would put paid to that. She had her health, or thought she had. Job could never be Job as long as he had that. Meanwhile, there was a life to live and a living to make, there was a family to keep and work to do – but always, at the end of work, thank God, there was ale.

For if Aunt Nonie was the fattest woman in the world, it was commonly agreed that what made her so was ale. No doubt it helped, as did the things that went with it: she never drank without singing and, when she sang, she put her heart and soul into it, which made a wild and pretty raucous noise. But that wasn't the real Aunt Nonie. Just follow her up from Hallo's one of those nights after she had downed the ale and sung her fill of songs and watch her moving about in the firelit gloom of the little hovel on Drummy's Lawn, with the black knitted shawl about her shoulders; or see her down at the stall on those nights coming up to Halloween when the lights came on and her shadow spread like some protecting spirit across the fruit. That was the real Aunt Nonie, the one who had to live on the few coppers that were left when the drinking and singing were done.

Anyway, in the end what they said came true: she did not 'call a halt', the ale was 'the livin' death of her', just like they said. It happened on an August Sunday morning and, when we went over, there she was, laid out in the brown habit of the Franciscans, with the Spanish galleon of a dresser loaded with fine china looking down on her and the creel of fruit she had swagged up from the stall the night before heaved in behind the door. The idea of her being dead was ridiculous. She couldn't be dead, not that great, great heart; there must be some mistake. A few minutes later, I'd be up and out of there, out in the sunlight and down the hill and there she'd be at the fountain, doing a roaring trade with the little juicy blood-oranges she could buy for half-nothing and sell at the handsome profit of a ha'penny apiece to all the kids making their way to the station for the Sea Breeze Excursion to Youghal that day.

And tonight she'd be back up, pulped from the heat but still unsuppressible, moving her great mound of resistance and good humour about the room, cursing the cat, letting the kettle boil over, burning the potatoes to the end of the pot, crooning, groaning, dozing in the basket-chair – anything, anything at all, but not dead, dressed up there like a painted doll in the finest suit she had worn since she was a bride.

And then someone pulled the cork from a bottle of stout and the drink was poured and drunk, and the women said, 'May the Lord have mercy on her soul'; but nobody sang. And with a swift, crushing, once-and-for-all-time certainty, then I knew: Aunt Nonie was dead. She had drunk her fill of ale and sung her fill of songs on August Saturday night; and now, God rest her merry soul – as her daughter Mary told us – 'she's payin' for it this mornin'!'

12

Braving it Out

AUNT Nonie was not alone. There were others like her, braving it out against death and destruction in the warrens of back-lanes around Shandon. Religion was a help to be sure: the Sacred Heart, Our Lady of Perpetual Succour, the gorgeous dolled-up Infant of Prague, Saint Anthony of the Child Jesus, later on the black St Martin de Porres, all those did their stint for us, called upon in Triduums and Novenas and Forty-Hours' to take a hand in our calamitous affairs. Debts, prison, unemployment, pawns, the dole – God and his saints must know those words well, in the singular sing-song accents of Cork. 'Is giorra cabhair Dé ná and doras' – God's help is nearer than the door indeed! But God was at a safe remove in Heaven, whereas for most of the time the door was an awful lot nearer.

Not just the burden of provision but the burden of prayer too fell mostly on the women. Nanny Apples once developed a tumour on her knee as big as a tennis-ball; those in the know said it was from all the kneeling she did in St Mary's on Pope's Quay. Later, when she got too old to kneel, I'd come on her sitting beside the window, mumbling and crooning her way through the rosary, praying for each and every one of us, children, grandchildren, even great-grandchildren, who probably had never even heard of her. A very mountain of cares to lay upon the Almighty, and that from but one of His afflicted souls in Cork.

The menfolk did not participate much. They would fill the church during the annual Mission, and maybe the odd night during the big liturgical occasions too, when a holy fervour would come alive in a brief gold rush upon the Confession-box and Holy Communion. That was the heyday of the Redemptorists and Passionists, great stentorian voices belting out hellfire and damnation. The Reverend Paisley up North missed his vocation by not being one of them!

And afterwards, during Benediction, with the smell of incense and the rise and fall of the Latin hymns in the air, we'd start dreaming about the dreadful things boys and girls got up to with each other – earthly bliss for the lucky ones who dared, but the fires of hell for all eternity if you dared too much.

Father rarely took any of this seriously. More by suggestion than by statement, he would let us know what he thought of it. Hadn't the 'Dubs' once sung 'Oh Parnellites, Oh Parnellites' for 'Oh Paradise, Oh Paradise' during a Christmas Mass in Palestine? Another time when Father Cummins, a local curate, down on his luck from drink and old age, came out to the altar with the chasuble all askew about his shoulders, to the great disgust of the parish 'ould wans', Father was in like a shot to his defence: 'I never read anywhere that the Almighty was a smart dresser. Can't they leave the poor chap alone? He's doin' the job he's paid to do. He'll be alright.'

But whether the men came or not, the women did

enough praying for them all. St Mary's on Pope's Quay was the heart and centre of our religious world and the white-robed Dominicans were all living saints, if the women could be believed. There was certainly enough devotional intensity around which was part-piety, part-spectacle, with the splendid painted ceilings inspiring high and holy thoughts. The Sistine Chapel has its imitators all over the world but none better than St Mary's.

As the smoke of incense rose above the packed pews and the organ swelled to the fervour of a hundred voices, you could be in no doubt that something very serious was afoot:

We stand for God and for His glory,
The Lord supreme and God of all.
Against His foes we raise our standards,
Around the Cross we hear His call.

Strengthen our faith, Redeemer,
Guard us when danger is nigh,
To Thee we pledge our lives in service,
Strong in a trust that ne'er shall die.
Strong in a trust that ne'er shall die

One way or another, we were all caught up in it but those who say the priests were its sole source and reason have it wrong. Mass and Confession apart, the priests had little enough to do with our daily lives. They certainly never came near us at home except to collect Christmas and Easter dues or when someone was dead. Furthermore, they belonged to a different class – a much more potent reason for the lack of contact. The truth is that we ourselves cross-fertilised each other, the mothers and grandmothers playing a primary role.

So when it is rumoured that the devil was seen in a house in Gurranabraher, we all rush up to have a ringside seat when the priest comes up to drive him out. It's bell, book and candle then and great-sounding Latin words to put the fear of God in the Evil One. The priest comes, a lot of holy water gets flung about and a lot of mumbo-jumbo gets said – but there's no sign of Old Nick at all. At least none we can see. Who knows, maybe he's still there; I wouldn't put it past them up in Gurrane! Religion can be a bit disappointing that way: an awful lot happening in the mind and the imagination, with the fires of hell and the choirs of angels all taken on trust – as I suppose they're meant to be.

Father is a natural-born sceptic when it comes to all that. Another night when word is out that the end of the world is nigh, we all rush up to the Cathedral at the top of Shandon Street, knowing that this means hell or heaven for us for all eternity. But if you pray hard enough, you could be saved. Well, it's good rough-and-ready theology, not much of it would I change. But, having done our stint in the Cathedral, we race down again; we're not Buck Jones or Hopalong Cassidy or Gene Autry now, there are graver things afoot. Up the dark stairs I go to our fourth-floor landing, not so afraid of Mad Annie and the howling cats, because there is worse at hand. The door opens above. It is Father going out on the night-shift at Kilbarry.

'Don't go out,' I beg him. 'Stay here at home.'

He looks at me, surprised at such urgent concern.

'Why? What's wrong?'

'They're all up in the Cathedral praying. It'll be the end of the world tonight.'

He walks past me out the door. But, as he goes he mumbles something that leaves me mystified.

'Jasus, boy,' he says, 'I wish it was.'

The world did not end, neither then nor at any other

time. Like the rest of us, I suppose it had developed the bad habit of going on and on and on. And it was the same old world as it had always been: the world of the slums and tenements, of drinking and brawling on Saturday nights, of raspberry and plum-pudding and the candle in the window at Christmas – and God's help being nearer than the door for the rest of the year; and pawns and loans, and new loans to keep up with the old ones – a galloping consumption that only death itself could bring to an end. For with death came that bonanza of the insurance policies, a magic wand to touch our world with gold and fill it with wonders till – puff! – the loot was gone and we were back to the old familiar hand-to-mouth again.

The policies were fine when the dead person was old; but with the young nothing could ever make good the loss. Tuberculosis was the worst killer; it ran in families. When it struck, it was like the Black Death, the whole lot going down in a single sheaf – households of seemingly healthy children all gone in the space of five or six years. The exceptions were the 'unlucky' ones who went away. When a boy or girl got a bad cough or bronchitis during the winter months, the dreaded word T.B. was never used; it just hung there in the air like the Grim Reaper with the scythe in the pictures of New Year's Eve.

There was a widespread ignorance about it which was truly shocking; even as a child, I recall wanting to scream with rage against its blind stupidity, against its doleful acceptance, with no redress but to weep and pray. One bad wetting or coming home in a sweat from a dance were sure-fire reasons for bringing down the curse. There would be a great nodding of heads then and much conspiratorial whispering as such reasons were discovered after the event; sudden unexplainable acts of God which were stoically

accepted, where good natural causes were not: bad food or
no food at all, damp and rotten beds, threadbare clothes in
the winter, three, four, five to a bed and no covering to speak
of – Christ in heaven, even a fool could see what brought it
on; why couldn't they?

One family up the road on Shandon Street slept under a
patchwork of newspapers – and then blamed the fumes from
Lunham's Bacon Factory for bringing T.B. into the house.
Inhaling such fumes was certain death.

Places like Dunlops' Tyre Factory and Ryan's Soap
Works had good jobs to offer, but the fumes from the melted
rubber or tallow were the beckoning hands of the Grim
Reaper. It was never T.B. – it was always 'something inward-
ly', 'a weakness', 'in a decline', 'outgrown his strength'. Like
a birthmark or the spells of witches, it was upon you, the
sign above the doorpost, the Destroying Angel from whom
none could get away.

So it was worse when someone used the word who
shouldn't, someone in authority who should know what it
meant, but could ignore it because, being poor, we were not
supposed to feel such things. Big sister Eily, our invalid, has
this flu; it hangs on for weeks and weeks till at last she can't
get out of bed and the doctor is called. He's the Dispensary
doctor, the nearly free-of-charge one, the only one we can
afford. It is the first time I have ever seen a doctor in the
house.

He's a great lumbering heap of a cattle-jobber with a
belly like a pregnant whale and a whale's face – not at all the
kind of appearance we're brought up to think a doctor
should have.

'Cough,' he tells our sister, which she does. 'Louder,' he
says, 'I can't hear you.' She coughs again, louder.

'How long has this gone on?' Mother tells him it's weeks,

whereat he turns on her and upbraids her for not calling him sooner.

'I didn't want to trouble you, Doctor.'

'More likely you thought to save the five shillings!' He tells our sister to put out her tongue and looks down her throat, then he puts this tube thing about his neck and into his ears and starts tapping her on the back and chest. Then he takes it off and goes bumbling down the stairs.

'What is it, Doctor?' Mother asks. 'Is it bad?'

'As bad as can be,' the bastard says. 'It's tuberculosis.'

A terrible fear grips us then and a look of helplessness and surrender passes between us and our death-sentenced girl. Characteristically, if there is a chink of hope, it has nothing to do with whether or not she has it, rather that 'there was never anything like that on our side of the family'.

And so we brave it out, in discreet and pitiable acceptance of a death that need not be a death, of the flower of our flock and the joy of our life snuffed out like a candle in the prime of her life.

> They brought her to the city
> And she faded slowly there;
> Consumption has no pity
> For blue eyes and golden hair.

That was us in Cork. Was it any different anywhere else? It would be years before I read the scene in Dostoevsky's *Crime and Punishment* where the mother spouts phthisic blood as she drags her contaminated children about the streets of Leningrad singing and playing wildly on the tambourine, begging kopeks from the rich on the Nevsky Prospect. It might just as well be the Grand Parade of Cork.

But there's a rage in the grace of God which is better

than the compliance which says 'Thy will be done' against so blind and summary a fate. Every life is a fight against the odds, but with T.B. you were somehow expected to accept the odds with equanimity. When you saw the pallor creep up the faces of those who had so short a time ago been young and beautiful, and when you saw helpless and distracted mothers reduced to lighting penny candles to Saint Anthony as a sole resort against their fate, then instead of 'Thy will be done' or 'Abandon hope, all ye who enter here', I would rather have Dylan Thomas' furious challenge:

> Do not go gentle into that good night,
> Rage, rage against the dying of the light.

As might be expected in this pale and sickly world, ghosts abounded. When the dark stairwell up to the fourth floor creaked or when a cat or rat scurried across your path, that was a ghost; and since ghosts could come from up or down, behind or before, there was no escape.

Then, when he's back from Curry's one Saturday night with Uncle Johnny, and the two of them get going with the war-talk, Father starts telling us about this ghost he saw in Africa.

'It was pitch dark and I was on sentry-go. I heard these footsteps coming towards me. "Halt!" I call, following the sentry rule-book, "Who goes there?" The steps keep coming, there is no reply.

'"Stand fast to be recognised," I call again. Still no response but the same footsteps.' At last, they are so close that he can see something. It's a ghost – so he lets fly with a single shot and hears the footsteps scurrying away.

'A bloody ghost to be sure,' Uncle Johnny confirms. 'I

often shot one of them meself and I on sentry-go in the war.'

Our eyes are out on sticks now. Mother, who has been fussing about, knows that there will be no sleeping for us in this house tonight. 'A lot of nonsense', she says. 'Ye ought to be ashamed of yeerselves saying things like that before the children. Ye know well there's no ghosts. Only the Holy Ghost.'

'She could be right, Johnny,' Father pulls back. 'I often thought it could have been some poor hoor of a kaffir out for a stroll before turning in for the night.'

'God, Kenny,' Johnny says. 'Is "kaffir" what they calls ghosts in Africa?'

'Shut up, Johnny,' Mother turns on him. 'I never heard such foolishness in me life. For grown men, ye haven't a tack o' sense. Ye'd be far better off to have yeer beads in yeer hand.'

But by now the damage is done. Her talk about 'no ghosts only the Holy Ghost' is fine while it's daylight but when the darkness comes down, it's different. Anyway, Mother is always saying things like that because she's the one who has to rescue us on the stairs when the ghosts are out. What she does not know is that Father and Uncle Johnny have a lively accomplice in the person of our own imagination. For the fact is that ghosts sometimes live in the very places where we live.

Across the road from us on Blarney Street lived our pal 'Baby' Looney. She died of T.B. when she was fifteen. The women all know it was T.B. but nobody says so; she was 'delicate', 'in a decline', 'had a bad chest' – anything and everything but that. She never played with us like the other girls and boys; just stood there to one side, tall, pale and gaunt, looking at the rest of us out of solemn sea-green eyes. When she died, she was laid out in the downstairs room and we all trooped in to see her.

She looked just as she did in life, only her eyes were closed and there were these two blonde plaits draped down over her shoulders, with the blue lace of the Child of Mary habit tying them up at the ends.

From then on, we have a real ghost to live with. Every creak on the stairs, every scurry of feet on the landing is Baby Looney come back to haunt us. It's no good now our mother saying things like 'There's no ghosts only the Holy Ghost' and 'What harm can she do ye? The innocent child is gone to a better place.' In the pitch dark we see Baby Looney's face on the landing – and we know that ghosts have only one purpose: to frighten the life out of us and turn us into ghosts like themselves.

Then, to cap it all, big brother Jim decides to take a hand and create a personal family ghost of our very own. This is 'The Dead Nun'. For hours on end, he will lie in wait on the stairs under a white sheet until it's time for us young ones to go to bed. Then, as we approach, he rises up under the sheet with the weirdest of weird sounds coming from him. If you have never seen a ghost, how can you tell that this is not one? Our younger sister Lil takes fright, the candle leaps from her hand and she goes flying down the stairs after it. It's ghost-time then alright, with her screaming and Jim howling, and Mother pounding the daylights out of him for his flight of fancy.

Another night, shortly after Baby Looney's death, I am coming down the road and I see this thing standing stock-still in the dark, right in the middle of my path. It is short and black and has no head. If it is not a ghost, what is it? Suddenly it lets out a scream.

'Timmy, are you comin' home at all tonight?'

I know the voice. It is our own Betsy, with the black shawl over her head. Her son Timmy and all of us would be far better off to meet a real ghost. No ghost could do a better job.

Snow-white sheets on a death-bed, white candles in candlesticks, fingers twined about a rosary beads – that's what a real ghost might look like. The deathly pallor of T.B. will be all around it – but then no one ever died of T.B.; it was all those other things. Paddy Kelly comes home from England for the funeral of his older brother Jim, a giant of a man who had 'outgrown his strength'.

'Poor Jim didn't last long,' one of his friends says, broaching the dreaded topic.

'Indeed he didn't,' Paddy concedes. 'He went very quick in the end.'

'What could it be at all, at all that took him so fast? It must have been bad, him going that fast and all.'

'Well, all I can say is that there was never anything like that on our side of the family. People go very fast these days.'

There is a silence while the topic dies.

'Of course he was always a bit on the delicate side.' Curiosity-killed-the-cat revives it. Still, brother Paddy is giving nothing away. But it has gone too far to stop now.

'What would you say yourself, Paddy? I mean, what would you say killed him?'

The grieving Paddy pushes his pint away and makes a final statement.

'Ah, I wouldn't know, I'm only just back. But whatever it was, it wasn't too serious anyway.'

In the midst of all this death and destruction, there is plenty of gaiety. The Hall at the top of Shandon Street, with its woodrot floor and woodworm seats, is a twopenny salve against the enveloping gloom; the Lido in Blackpool is a classier one at threepence; the Assembly Rooms on the South Mall – Friends Meeting House by day, cinema by night – is fourpenceworth of wonders.

'Hoppy' in the Hall, 'Lulu' in the Lido, 'Bundle' in 'The Assems' – they are all gods in their own right, the arclight from their torches sweeping across our rapt faces when the going gets rough on the screen and, with missiles of all sorts, we take direct action to help our imperilled heroes.

Or, when the urgent yelps and screams from the plush seats behind tell Hoppy and Lulu and Bundle that action of another kind is afoot, there is not much they will be able to do to rescue those damsels in distress!

Then one year big sister Eily sees this advertisement in the *Echo* for a bungalow to let in Crosshaven: ten shillings a week in August. It's a fortune but we make it. Off down we troop in style to catch the first bus on August Sunday morning with pots and pans, cups, saucers, every tool and tittle known to God and man – and enough loaves and fishes along with them to feed 5,000! We're prospectors on our way to a gold rush; we're in The Himalayas on our way to Shangri-la, Mother leading the pack. Father stays at home. She's out in style in hat and coat with the fox fur about her neck and the cute little fox's eyes looking back at the rest of us following behind. On the bus-ride to 'Crosser', names of pure magic come up with the milestones: Carrigaline, Fountainstown, Myrtleville, Robertscove; then at last, rounding the last bend, a thousand slim pillars against the skyline, the Royal Yacht Club of Crosshaven, ancient bastion of the rich and famous, bidding an airy welcome to the hoi polloi of Cork.

Our 'Shangri-la' is 'Edith', a two-roomed wooden shack with a stove in one corner, a home-grown table and chairs in another, and bunks and mattresses stashed against the bedroom walls. 'At least we'll be dry when the rain comes,' Mother says, as always looking on the bright side.

For once, the rain does not come. Crosshaven on that one week is like those places we read about in *Film Fun* – Coney Island and Palm Beach – where from dawn to dusk they live in naked splendour through the sun-kissed days. At the end of each of those seven days, as the sun goes down behind the hills, we make our way to Piper's Merry-Go-Round and the miracle happens again: at the roulette-table, pennies drop like manna from heaven, big brother Jim gets more of them to drop at the slot-machines. So it's ice-cream and Kit-Kats for us younger ones – for hours everlasting 'the Vanderbilts have asked us out to tea!' And, boy oh boy, are we coming!

All day long, Lil and I are out on the strand in sunsuits run up for us by big sister Eily on the old clickety-clack machine. Big brother Ken, as always the provider, fishes mackerel out of the frothing inlets between the rocks; and Jim, never missing a chance to distinguish himself, daily presents us with fine new potatoes from some nearby field, his personal *droit de seigneur*, from an unsuspecting farmer!

Come Saturday night and the week is nearly up. Suddenly, through the dark on the gravel outside, we hear someone stumble and there is singing. From the song we know who it is:

> Bravely fought upon the Glencoe Heights,
> Put five thousand crafty Boers to flight;
> It was a grand, a glorious sight –
> Bravo, the Dublin Fusiliers.

Father, down for the weekend, has brought a cooked ham

wrapped in a towel, a gallon jar of Guinness, lemonade and bull's-eyes – and, to cap it all, a Thomson's cake for Mother, the ultimate peace offering. Oh, shall we then cull out a holiday and shall we then strew flowers in his way! Because now, with Father, Mother and all of us there, we are the sole owners of the whole world. And all for ten-bob in a wooden shack. Who would have thought the world could come so cheap?

My eyelids droop. I am falling asleep. At last someone lifts me up to the top bunk against the bedroom wall. I lie there listening to the Atlantic crashing against the rocks of Church Bay, with the Cyclops Eye of the Weavers' Point Lighthouse sweeping past the window like the sweep of an angel's wings. If I had known how, I would have thanked God then for being a small boy in a poor house, the last of a lost but not a lonely tribe. On this once at least did the meek inherit the earth. And the ten-shilling spendthrifts of this world were wiser in their generation than the Vanderbilts of light.

13

'I was Sad to Leave it All Behind me'

THE time is coming when I will leave all this behind me, but it is not yet. There is still a way to go and there are still some things to do. One of them is to be a milkman's boy and quite happy to go on being that for all time to come. Others had done the like before me: just left school as soon as they could and got a job, any job that was going – why not me? Messenger-boys, hod-carriers, sweeping the clippings from the floors of the Lee Boot Factory or Metal Products – if they were lucky, maybe become apprentices to their fathers' trades. It was that or the *Innisfallen*, our haughty conquistador sailing down the Lee with the dropping tide past the rusty hulks stuck in the mud, like some of our schoolmates that were stuck in another way. For those who stayed, the object was to be able to earn enough to be able to buy a packet of Woodbines or go to the pictures on the weekend nights, a blind, terminal life buffered and succoured by such small rewards. It was no good blaming the parents. The only difference between them and the children was that they in their time had done the same, only younger and for less.

Our own father had left school finally at the age of eight. Our mother never spoke about school at all; years later, when she had to sign her name to something, she would put down an 'X' and the clerk would write 'Her Mark'. This would make me blush with shame and I laboured through long hours trying to teach her; in the end, she could manage the 'Julia' well enough but the surname was beyond her. 'Bad luck to me schoolmistress,' she'd say; the miracle of those spidery lines making up into a name would never be achieved now. In this, she was no different from most other women about the place; but she was unique in her insistence that none of us would be like that. It is hard to say where the education thing came from, though clearly our unschooled but intelligent father must have gained some notion of what it could do from his years in foreign parts. And Mother would have picked this up in a way that made the triple leap from hope through work to the grand rewards of the permanent and pensionable.

And then there were the Christian Brothers. They took vows of poverty, chastity and obedience, poverty being the most important from our point of view because they could surely never expect anything from us.

They carried about with them an invisible trinity of virtues: godliness, national fervour and a scrubbed and Calvinistic sense of discipline which was wholly approved, by mothers especially, as an essential ingredient for advancement to the good life. If a boy bucked the Brothers, he was in for a rough time. Parents acquiesced, hoping that school alone would do the trick. But even then, if you were at all aware, you could see that a great deal of what became of you depended on yourself. A lot of horses were brought to the water in those years, but most of them refused to drink. The stock response – 'Why would he be wastin' his time with oul' books in school, when he could be out earnin'?' – paid no heed to the notion of learning for its own sake. That was unheard of – a folly and a blasphemy against the God-given need to find money to keep body and soul together.

The money for the milkman's helper I became was six-pence a week, a small fortune for someone who had never seen sixpence together in his life before. It was a tough old station: up at seven to run the milk-round with the two-gal-lon can and the pint measure until it was time for school; in summer, that happened twice a day, so it was away again to do the second half of the round as soon as school was over.

But it wasn't the dawn rising or the running all over the place with the two-gallon can, and it certainly wasn't the 'tanner', though that counted too; it was the thrill of being left to tackle and untackle the horse, of being given the reins and feeling the strong pull of the young cob run-ning between the shafts, with neither books nor school nor future nor past nor any other thing at all to think about but the all-consuming passion of real life of now.

The farm is five miles out over the top of Farmers' Cross where Cork Airport now is. It has a cobbled yard and when I drive the horse and cart across the cobbles at mid-day, it makes a grand sound like a giant rollicking with delight. Then I unyoke the sweating cob and lead him to the stables where there's a smell of fresh-cut mangolds and new-mown hay. In winter, steaming plumes of white breath fan out from the nostrils of the other horses as they champ and trample on the trodden straw.

On Sundays, I get to play hurling with the other men and boys about the place and, when we come in, the dairy is the place to go, a white-washed shed, ice-cold, with no light but the light from the open door and the gleaming churns standing about. If you are thirsty, and I always am, you dip a cup in the churn and swallow the icy cream, smooth as ivory and heaven's bliss to a twelve-year-old animal boy.

When I come home on Sunday nights, there is the home-work untouched since Friday. It is waiting in the schoolbag beside the door, a leaden load I do not want to know. I see and want nothing then but to be back on my Sabine farm, a milkman's boy at a 'tanner' a week, with the long-term ambition that one day I might become a milkman myself, with my own horse and cart and my very own milk-round, the monarch of all I survey as I sit atop my coloured cart, wanting nothing more in the world for all time to come.

That is a time before I was born, when my world is a world of animals and farmyards, the reek of horses and the swish of milk in the milking-pails, the sudsy white liquid splashing around all day long in my two-gallon can. My best ambition, if I have one, is to be able to tackle or untackle a horse faster than any of the hired hands about the place.

Could I have stayed that way? Could I have gone on and grown like that to be a man? Was there another me inside the me I became, someone who got lost along the way and was never heard of again?

I do not think so. Is there any life but the life we live, any choice but the choice we make? All I know is that there was a time when that was as real as anything now is real and I was a different me from the me I am now. With wonder and bewilderment, I ask myself – what miracle of events would bring such changes about? For it would all stop suddenly one day, and from then on I would go a different way.

But for now, after my morning milk-run, it was up and away from Turner's Cross on the south side to the Christian Brothers in Blarney Street on the north where my brothers, Ken, Jim and John went before me. On the Rock Steps, wild valerian sprouts from the limestone walls, white and pink and crimson, hectic and very beautiful but, alas, born to blush unseen and waste its sweetness on the North Side air!

The Brothers knew our mother well and recognised in her the true object of their vocational zeal: the poor but dauntless Mother Machree struggling against death and damnation to bring her brood to a better life. There is a sense in which she actually loved them; a love three parts gratitude for their service free of charge and one part regret that, even if she wanted to, there was no way she could pay. To her dying day, she would go into raptures about them; and when, later in life, she developed a most unlikely passion for the game of hurling, it was nothing to do with the game at all but rather that it was the game the Christian Brothers' boys excelled at, including big brother Ken's pals, the Lynch brothers, especially Jack, whom she loved as if they were her own.

There was no charge for primary school, just a few pounds a year for secondary – and if there was real need, the Brothers would waive that. Even more, in really desperate circumstances, they would quietly see to it that the boys were clothed and fed. Yes, there were abuses – the 'strap' was everywhere, some lads had a devilish knack of drawing trouble on themselves. And, covert and unspoken as it was, there was indeed sexual carry-on, inevitable in those celibate lives. But by and large the Brothers were a beacon of hope in a dark time, the one chance we had of some day coming out of that darkness into a new and better life.

A new Head Brother comes to 'Blarney-a'; he has the name of being a bad egg. Small, bald and fat, with the lips of a lover who has never known love, 'Bonty' comes at us with the brand of the destroying angel to scourge our small lives with taunt, belittlement and derision. This, backed by the power of terrifying rages, soon makes him a nightmare in the land. As I cross the city each morning to the acrid smell of hops brewing in the vats of Beamish's, its reek becomes the reek of fear and dread of another day. Boys literally flee the place when Bonty comes at them: Paddy Foran, agile and tall beyond his years, manages to scramble through the window and jump out onto the street in the nick of time before the destroying angel descends; he never comes to school again.

Willie John Cooney, seeing him come at his younger brother with the dreaded strap aloft, grabs him from behind and gets him out the door before the evil one can reach them. That's the last we see of them. But Bonty's aim is clear: it is to achieve a name and fame for his slum-school amidst the lanes of 'Blarney-a', to make scholars out of at least some few of its squalid and half-starved weans. Of this select but menaced few, I will be one.

After school each day when the others have gone, he puts us through two, three hours more of grinding work. There we sit in the classroom dusk, a brave new world of slum-cleared improvers, listening to the blackbirds in the Brothers' orchard and, beyond the walls, the shouts of our liberated classmates playing soccer in the street outside; while a whole world of new names and new words begins to be born: factors and rectangles, tangents and square-roots, Shelley, Milton, Keats – all ducking and diving like the sparrows and starlings under the eaves on the narrow lanes off Blarney Street.

Spring comes and the wild valerian on the Rock Steps bursts into bloom. The scholarships exam is at Easter and, like the yearling hopefuls we now are, we are rearing to go. All the soaked-up knowledge, all the facts and figures, the data, dates and dimensions, the words, the syntax and the grammar-rules – it all comes out in a dozen crammed hours that will set the course of our future lives. It's a race to be sure, a race to be won. And, as we run, we pray to God for the luck or fortune to end up in the first ten past the finishing post.

That's Easter. By the following August I have long forgotten those early spring days. Then on Friday before the August weekend, there's this flurry in the street outside and someone comes banging at the door. Mother goes to open it; it's a pal from up the road.

'Mrs Murphy ... Mrs Murphy ... there's a –'

'Take it easy, boy, draw your breath.'

'But this man ... up the road ... is in the Corporation ... and he's just after tellin' us –'

'Tellin' ye what? It must be terrible bad to have you in a state like this.'

'He's after tellin' us –'

'What?'

'That a "William Murphy" is after gettin' first place in the City Scholarship.'

Promptly I go off to the City Hall to inquire. There is this big red ledger which the clerk takes from his desk and lays it out before me. And there indeed it is: Murphy, William, the first name on the list. That old grandfather William – the one who could tell how many times the clock ticked in a year – must have turned in his grave. Maybe there is such a thing as passing on the gift after all!

So the course of my star is set. I move to a new school, still the Christian Brothers – this time, the North Monastery near Farrenferris. I'm the only one from 'Blarney-a' to go there. Each day now I pass Winnie and Willie's tenement where I first saw the light of day; sometimes I take a look to see if they are still there: the ageing childless couple begging us to come in – luring us to destruction with bread and marmalade; Miss Goggin, pale and powdered behind her veil; Mad Annie peering into the stairwell in pursuit of her night-prowling cats. I have no fear of them now; I am fifteen and have put such fears behind me. I am an adult; what's more an educated adult. And the bright new world is opening up before me.

The lanes off Shandon Street and Blarney Street are still there at that time, grimy with smoke from the tottering chimneys and the dross of lifetimes flowing into the drains. Shell-shocked Uncle Timmy with his pipe and his silences; his sister, Aunt Nonie, 'the fat woman at the fountain' – they still hold out amidst the cobbles and crumbling moss-stones of Drummy's Lawn. And on New Year's Eve at Shandon, it's still the same: 'the bells are ringing the old year out and the New Year in.' And with each year of them, the people come and go, the births, deaths and marriages that mark the days, weeks and years of our passing humdrum lives.

But there are sea-changes in the map at home. At a party or at the end of one of those fortune-telling nights, our invalid sister Eily will dance the hornpipe to everyone's delight – holding onto a chair on each side as a prop to support her – but especially to the delight on one 'Fox', a red-haired hero from up the road, captain of our 'Celtic' soccer team and a Paul Robeson when it comes to singing 'Ole Man River'. There are long nights when the two of them are closeted together in 'The Room', with John McCormack and His Master's Voice shut off, and much whispering and occasional furious giggling to fill the curious silence.

Then one night she comes out and she has this ring on, and there's great oooh-ing and aaah-ing and Father solemnly shakes hands with 'Fox' and calls Eily 'his little star' and gallon jars of stout are brought in and there's much kissing and crying until at last Father calls a halt to 'all this bloody oul' nonsense' and can we have something to bring us down to earth? Which we do: it's 'Bravo, the Dublin Fusiliers'.

Next, it's big brother Ken's turn. He is the bicycle-in-the-hallway man – only well-got ladies will do for him. There's a run of them to be sure, again with tea and cakes served up to them in 'The Room', doyleys on the table and us young ones forbidden under pain of death to burst in. We don't know who the ladies are but, when we see them through the curtains coming up the road, they look very fine indeed, all paint and powder and speaking in the grand accents of Cork. But they come and they go and then 'The Room' is silent again.

Until at last he brings us Peg, 'lovely and fair like the roses of summer'. What's more, Mother likes her – a crucial plus in our matriarchal world. This time the lady stays. He still has the bicycle in the hallway – the white-collars are still white, the pensions as permanent as ever. So off they go and have a life of it; it's no longer our life, though through all the years he never ceases to be our beacon and our path-finder, the Moses who led us out of our slum-room bondage into the Promised Land.

Wild brother Jim does what he's always done: torments the living daylights out of everyone, friends and neighbours as well as ourselves, until we're all at loggerheads with him and them. All except Mother, who won't have a cross word said against him. He doesn't bring any women home, which may be just as well because no woman will ever look after him the way his mother does. After he ran away and joined the Army, he's sitting at the fire at home toasting his shins one Christmas – having toasted his insides the night before – when Mother finds time in the midst of her twelve-handed chores to bring him a bottle of stout and a ham-sandwich to keep his spirits up.

'That's how we do things in the Army,' the purring cat-kind announces. 'Look after yourself and you'll never want for anything.'

Jim's haunt is the Central Ballroom near Patrick's Bridge – a 'tanner' to get in and the males won't darken the door till they're stocious with drink and can barely see the painted hopefuls stacked against the females wall. It's on the quays where the ships come in laden with birds – as if there weren't enough of them already onshore. For the assembled talent, then, it will be a short sharp shore-leave with a plentiful supply of love-letters to smooth the way – and we are not talking about the written kind.

Somehow, by some miracle of mother-love, Jim is spared the worst ravages of the Central and in due course finds himself more seriously engaged. She too is Peg, a petite 'femme fatale' with the jet-black hair of the opera heroine Carmen, like her mother before her. A Carmen indeed she is, a deep contralto like her opera namesake, who sang in the chorus of the Cork Opera House and never after lets us forget it. In this, English Victorian manners spilt over to holy Catholic Ireland, according to which a woman who went on stage could not be a right woman; the harlequin, the harlot and the chorus-girl were all tarred and feathered with the same black brush. But Jim's Peg put paid to all that, took Mother's pride and joy in hand and made a life for him – side by side with the booze, the horses and the hurling, a triad of second strings to his mercurial bow; and mothered him five children, all in the same mould, the living image of her – and faithful as their father in defence of everything that could remotely be called their own.

One such possession which they can certainly call their own is his residue of old schoolbooks. These are produced half a lifetime later to become an abiding link with his unscholarly past and a live treasure-trove, now that there is no longer a school and Christian Brothers to rebel against. And not just him but the children too, as he leads them through the intricacies of algebra and geometry, quadratic equations and the binomial theorem, not to mind his fine sonorous renditions of Satan and Beelzebub from *Paradise Lost* and his haunted version of the broken Macbeth telling them that 'Tomorrow, and tomorrow, and tomorrow, Creeps in this petty pace from day to day'.

Oh, he could have been a scholar alright, our wayward brother Jim, if he had put his mind to it. In his case learning was for its own sake, a salve and a palliative against the shipwreck of his later life. Maybe in some corner of heaven where he surely is, there is a rough-house to accommodate his turbulent will and lively mind. There, he'll have the scope he needed but never got to be the ever-youthful learner, even the good teacher he could have been, if only his errant star had guided him in other ways.

I leave him with a memory of the last time I saw him. He is with his youngest daughter, a little girl of twelve, and they are spouting words and phrases at each other in a language I do not know. It turns out to be Russian – the language of Pushkin, Turgenev, Tolstoy – the Linguaphone disc running beside them to chart their studious way. Did the authors of that audio-disc ever dream they would have such unlikely learners?

And last of all, there's Lil. (I speak here only of those who are gone; brother John is still around, the nearest of the boys to me in age and the one I have been closest to all my life. So close indeed that he, not I, might have written this. Maybe in time – but not too soon, I hope! – he will add the final piece; the one about me!)

But for now Lil. She is our younger sister, just two years ahead of me and, from infancy, my special pal. 'He-eye-dee-open' she is reputed to have said when she looked in over the cotside and saw me open my eyes for the first time upon the light of day. It is a thousand years away in time and a thousand songs of experience will be sung before I look in over a cotside at her, as she closed her eyes forever upon her light of day. In the meantime, she is another of Father's 'little stars' and brings the glitter of stars into our house. In her teens she's big into dances and dance-halls; a little later, we discover that she has this love-ly soprano voice, a voice of perfect pitch and clarity. Time after time she will stun us to silence with Abba's 'I Had a Dream', Handel's 'Did You Not See My Lady?' and our own Irish songs, 'Carrigdown' and 'The Dawning of the Day'. We had neither the money nor the thought for it – what might she not have come to if she had had some training? But such might-have-beens are a treachery upon the one life we live, a wishful thinking for a path we shall never know.

The path we do know brings us Dan, a bus-conductor in London but home on holiday in Cork when he hears her singing and she hears him; he has Bing Crosby's voice and looks like Bing with his lovely easygoing smile. Mother shortly informs us that 'she's very much taken up with him'. London is left to its own devices and Dan soon becomes an item around the house.

He moves about with muscular ease, crooning the lullabies of Bing without any frills or flounces, just a steady soothing flow, much to our Mother's liking. So Lil may have her way – and deserve it.

For she is the one who never got a chance at all: started at fourteen in the bacon factory on Evergreen to help keep the home-fires burning after Father died. In this, as in everything, I owe her a great deal; the first pair of shoes I would ever wear, bought with a goodly half of her First Communion money; several bloody noses which taught me to respect the rage of girls when they're crossed; how to laugh when you could cry and how to shut up and say nothing when there is nothing you can do to change whatever you have to cry about.

All this happened while we explored the green-shoot world about us: first mates to each other in many daring ventures: climbing the sally-trees out the Black Ash; fingering the iron ring set in the oak-tree where Red Riding Hood was held while the wolf prowled in the nearby woods; stealing the daffodils and bluebells from the Bishop's Field to bring them home for the May altar, while the alsatian bayed at us beyond the barred gate. As child, as boy, as man – Dan or no Dan – she will be with me till the day she dies.

That is light-years away now and means nothing to us. For now we are in a world of skipping-ropes and daisy-chains, of hopscotch on the footpath chalk-marked with broken heads of the Blessed Virgin and the Sacred Heart, skating on slides belted out on the roadway to the screams of Betsy and the terror of carthorse-and-driver trying to skate up: the Pipes of Pan and the songs of innocence that will go on from here through all eternity:

Wallflowers, wallflowers, growing up so high,
All pretty children never going to die,

Except Lily Murphy, she's the only one,
She can sing and she can dance and she can turn her back to
   the wall.

It is all but over, the clock is ticking, the time is up. But there
is yet one prize to come, that bicycle-in-the-hallway; there can
be no stopping until that is won. So it's the daily trek across
the city and up Shandon Street to the Christian Brothers at the
North Mon. I am all alone in the house with Mother now;
Father is dead, the others are all at work or married or gone
away. She is barely aware of me: my comings and goings are
her one clock. Out of some primal sense of order, she starts
out of her amnesia to do the things that must be done when I
arrive. I am seventeen now but my eyelids droop in soporific
unison and I drop off to sleep at the table, head down on my
arms. When I come to, there she is at the window, looking out
blindly across the street for the days and times that will not
come again. But even these last times will come and go too,
as everything and everyone must, down the relentless con-
veyor-belt in this abattoir of a life.

I make it to the winning-post, I get my white collar job,
the die is cast. My bicycle-in-the-hallway will pedal this second postulant for fame to that new and higher life.

Big brother Ken is there to see me off from Glanmire
Railway Station, the starting point for the big bad world from
the pink and pearly refuge of Cork. He doesn't want me to
leave; he has had a dozen years of civil servitude behind him
by now; he knows that white collars can choke and that a
bicycle-in-the-hallway can fetch you up in strange places
where you never wanted to be. But how do you say such
things to someone who does not want to hear?

'So, I'm off to Dublin in the green, in the green' – it is the
end of the road. We wave each other goodbye and the train
pulls out. The dark tunnel from Glanmire is a 'fade-to-black'

long enough to create a new scene at the far end. I am on my own now, with a single suitcase full of my life's belongings – with all my worldly goods I thee endow! Well, alone is where we start, alone is where we end, in a world peopled by bipeds, all of us strangers to each other, but for our one safe cocoon, our one nest – our home.

EPILOGUE

There are warm lights inside the grand houses coming up towards Dublin's Lansdowne Road, the fires are lighting and there are happy people talking to each other inside. It is a cosy and expensive world of which I am not a part.

I am an outsider, a stray molecule cut loose from its nucleus, floating without sense or purpose out in space. My nucleus is miles away – in the two-pair back of a tenement house on Blarney Street, in the cramped kitchen of a Council house in Turners Cross, where a bewildered woman is wondering what has become of her frantic life, when there is no one about to care for anymore.

I close my eyes and, in that still-frame moment, I am back with them. All is as it used to be: invalid Eily dancing the hornpipe, holding onto the chairs; ardent Ken bent above his books to the hiss of the paraffin-lamp; turbulent Jim spoiling for a fight; Father, Mother, Lil – their 'little star' – singing the songs of innocence; John and me, now sole survivors clinging to the wreckage.

It is a wordless moment and will pass. But can it ever pass?

Never.

Because its name is eternity. And the wordless word that hangs in the air unspoken there is – love.